A USEFUL HISTORY OF BRITAIN

MICHAEL BRADDICK

A USEFUL
HISTORY OF
BRITAIN

The Politics of Getting Things Done

OXFORD
UNIVERSITY PRESS

Great Clarendon Street, Oxford, OX2 6DP,
United Kingdom

Oxford University Press is a department of the University of Oxford.
It furthers the University's objective of excellence in research, scholarship,
and education by publishing worldwide. Oxford is a registered trade mark of
Oxford University Press in the UK and in certain other countries

First Edition published in 2021

Impression: 1

Published in the United States of America by Oxford University Press
198 Madison Avenue, New York, NY 10016, United States of America

British Library Cataloguing in Publication Data
Data available

Library of Congress Control Number: 2021935503

ISBN 978-0-19-884830-1

Printed and bound by
CPI Group (UK) Ltd, Croydon, CR0 4YY

For Sarah

ACKNOWLEDGEMENTS

As ever, I am grateful for the stimulating intellectual community at the University of Sheffield but in this case especially to my colleagues in SCEMS for allowing me the chance to try out the arguments as I was finishing the book. I am also indebted to Scott Ashley, Dan Beaver, John Moreland, Julia Moses, Luciana O'Flaherty, Jill Pritchard, and Chris Wickham who read drafts of the book: it is much improved as a consequence. For advice on particular matters, and more general encouragement, I am grateful to Adrian Bingham, Dominic de Cogan, Masashi Haneda, Eliza Hartrich, Ian Mason, Paul Slack, John Snape, John Walter, John Watts, and Charles West. Katharine Braddick read a part of the book and listened to me talk about some of its ambitions. Mark Greengrass pointed me towards the Marc Bloch quotation which appears as an epigraph.

Finally, some more personal thanks: to Minnie, who encouraged me to buy a book about Sutton Hoo, and to Cora and Mel who showed polite and helpful interest. Above all, though, I am more grateful than I can say to Sarah for her love and support in this, as in so much else.

CONTENTS

CONTENTS

LIST OF ILLUSTRATIONS

Misunderstanding of the present is the inevitable consequence of ignorance of the past. But a man may wear himself out just as fruitlessly in seeking to understand the past, if he is totally ignorant of the present.

Marc Bloch, *The Historian's Craft* (Manchester, 1979 edn), p. 43

INTRODUCTION

*From Stonehenge to Global Britain: The History
of Political Life on Britain*

Humans have probably been on what is now Britain for around 900,000 years. For the vast bulk of that time they lived by hunting and gathering, retreating south for long periods when the ice advanced. The evidence of their lives is largely restricted to their tools, traces of their camps, the bones of the animals they ate. The oldest human remains are about 500,000 years old and, towards the end of this very long period, we have traces of human art, but there is very little evidence of the collective life of these people. About 6,000 years ago, however, this changed very rapidly. The widespread adoption of farming resulted in more settled societies that left a much clearer mark on the landscape. That evidence reveals almost immediately that late Neolithic (or Late Stone Age) societies were capable of spectacular collective action.

Over the intervening 6,000 years people have acted together in a great variety of ways to address many different challenges, leaving a wealth of evidence about their collective action. So what might we learn from this vast store of experience? This is a critical question given the tone of much current political discussion, which is often pessimistic about our ability to meet collective challenges such as climate change, pandemics, or managing the global economy. We have not benefited from the full range of this past experience, however, because conventional histories of Britain tend to focus on the origins of the UK and British national identity. This book asks a simple but very different question: what can we learn by thinking about how people in the past acted together to get things done?

*　　*　　*

Some of the collective achievements of the late Neolithic are truly remarkable. At Avebury in Wiltshire, for example, several square miles have been transformed into a ritual landscape of impressive scale including a henge (circular ditch, bank, and stone circle) and a huge mound, Silbury Hill: testament to the transformative potential of collective action. Silbury Hill is 30 metres high and 160 metres wide, the largest such earthwork in Europe, and probably dates from around 2400 BCE. It is estimated that moving the half a million tons of material it contains would have required 4 million person hours of work (perhaps 1,000 people working for two years, supported by many others?). The full transformation we can now see around Avebury must have required the mobilization and coordination of labour on a very large scale over several generations and there is evidence of several stages of design and re-design. Across the Salisbury plain, at Stonehenge, similarly remarkable re-organization of the landscape took place. Here the scale of organization reached far beyond the immediate environs, not least in the stone settings, which date from around 2500 BCE. Sixty or so bluestones, each weighing between 2 and 5 tons, were brought to the site from south-west Wales. The larger sarsens, the biggest of which weighs 30 tons, were brought at least 25 km.

Confronted by these remains, it is natural to wonder how it was done. The scale of the achievement seems incredible given the popular view of Stone Age societies, but these transformations were clearly the product of complex societies with considerable organizational capacity. We have no real idea who coordinated this effort—which individual or group—or how they mobilized the necessary labour. We assume that this was a society in which some individuals had greater power than others, but in the absence of evidence we really know very little about it: it is hard to say, for example, whether it was done cooperatively, coordinated by people acting consensually in an egalitarian way, or by command of people who dominated their society.

In later periods we can say much more about that and it is often helpful to think about power along two axes: firstly, as the collective capacity to, for example, build henges; and, secondly, as a relationship between those with the power to coordinate, control, and command and those without it. Political life, in other words, gives us power over our social and material world, but also power over each other. Much of political history can be understood in these terms, as a dialogue between the *collective* power to achieve things together, and the *differential* power of those in control or coordinating positions. It is, for example, a way of understanding much about the history of kings, priests, prime ministers, parliaments, and tax officials.

As well as asking how it was done, visitors wonder why it was done *there*: what was special about that place? That is a hard question to answer, perhaps impossible. However, the site does illustrate another general feature of political history: that past decisions shape future action, in a process called *path dependency*. There is evidence that this particular place had a ritual significance much longer ago, perhaps before farming came to the island. We are certain that not long after the arrival of farming, from around 5,500 years ago, it was redeveloped in several phases: once something was placed there, it became a reason to continue to use that site. Asking when Stonehenge was built is a bit like asking when London was built, in other words—it was a site that was continually developed and re-developed, in fact over a far longer period than London has been there. But if we cannot say with any certainty why this place was special, we can say that once it had become recognized as such, later generations had reason to use it. This is an important aspect of political history—how decisions taken at one point create a path dependency which shapes action in the future.

For most modern visitors the question of *how* Stonehenge was built jostles for attention with the question of *why* it was built. Here we have some quite good answers. The henge is clearly aligned with the movements of the sun, for example, and the large numbers of pigs' teeth found at the site are all from animals of an age that suggests they were slaughtered at mid-winter. In fact, the scientific and interpretive brilliance of work on the site means we have a better glimpse of the mobilizing ideas that produced Stonehenge than of the social and political organization which made it possible, or the path dependency that placed those massive stones at that particular place.

We can also say something about the geography of the culture in which it stood. There are strong connections between Stonehenge and associated or similar remains elsewhere. The wider archaeological record reveals clear links between continental Europe and south-east Britain and between western Britain and the European Atlantic seaboard. It is also clear that by this time influence could spread southwards too. Domestic architecture seems to link the buildings in the area around Stonehenge with those at Skara Brae in the Orkneys, while the megalithic ritual architecture seems to have been adopted earlier at the Ness of Brodgar than at Stonehenge, and therefore to have spread southwards. On the other hand, the later burial at Stonehenge of the 'Amesbury archer', a man who grew up in Alpine Europe, suggests that it was an important site or resource for people in the south too. In any case it is clearly a site which connected the lives of people living far apart, and not just on Britain. It offers a rare glimpse of a Neolithic culture with much more than local significance.

Stonehenge has a wider context not just through these cultural connections (a shared history) but also as an index of a parallel history. This form of construction—circular banks and ditches enclosing a stone circle—seems to have been distinctive to Britain, but the construction techniques were not. Megalith building was widespread in this period, reflecting a shared technological capacity, although not necessarily a shared pattern of social organization or world view. The same techniques were used to construct different architectural forms that might have expressed quite different beliefs. In that sense it is a parallel, as much as a shared history, defined by similar levels of technological and organizational capacity: the ability to use stone in this way, and the ability to organize labour on the necessary scale.

As we have seen, the capacity to construct on this scale is associated with the emergence of agricultural societies—the common assumption being that only human groups which had abandoned hunting and gathering had the capacity (and perhaps will) to undertake such projects. Farming and trade are associated with a more complex division of labour and the movement of goods. The many person hours devoted to projects like those at Stonehenge and Avebury had somehow to be supported—at the very least there must have been surplus food production, and a population able to live on that surplus and undertake other tasks. Farming greatly facilitated this kind of collective action.

This again illustrates a more general feature of political history: that new skills and trades make new forms of collective action possible. For example, the invention of printing created new possibilities for governments in the sixteenth century, allowing the dissemination of standardized information, or the gathering of information in a standardized form. Similarly, the advent of the internet has created the possibility of closer and more intimate political communication, as well as surveillance. Facial recognition software, in fact, is thought to be such a dangerous thing in the hands of political authorities that in 2019 the City of San Francisco banned its use by public agencies. In both cases new technologies developing independently of government have facilitated changes in political ambition. The opposite is also true, that collective organization makes new forms of economic activity possible. Thus, the creation and the storage of written records by government in the tenth and eleventh centuries increased the demand for scribes and fostered the development of new skills in making, storing, and retrieving information which were then taken up by private individuals and groups.

Although economic and political organization are closely related, however, they are fundamentally different. Collective power is consciously directed and coordinated; economic complexity is in principle self-organizing. In theory it arises from the choices made by individuals or groups, who exchange with others: farmers, blacksmiths, millers, bakers, shoemakers, and so on.

The result is a great variety of mutually dependent and specialized employments which no one has planned; it is the aggregate effect of individual decisions, rather than the working out of an overall plan or intelligent design. To return to the Stonehenge example, it certainly seems unlikely that it was a product of self-organizing activity, arising organically from myriad individual decisions and actions. That the plan could be made and implemented, however, seems to have depended on economic complexity: it was distinctively a product of agrarian not hunter-gathering society.

Explaining Stonehenge involves thinking about collective organization, mobilizing ideas, the geography of power and identity, the interrelationship of collective power, economic complexity, and technological capacity; and also about how these things are part of a wider shared history or had parallels elsewhere. It is now British in the sense that it is in the UK and on land inhabited by people who identify as, among other things, Britons. However, it is extremely unlikely that saying so would have meant much to the people who built it, or that there is much institutional or cultural continuity between them and modern Britons. The current inhabitants of Britain are connected with the builders of Stonehenge much more directly by the way they use collective power than by the history of particular national institutions or collective identity. The premise of this book is that there is more to learn by thinking about their experience of acting collectively than about their contribution to the making of the UK and modern British identity.

*   *   *

Understanding how people have got things done in the past may sound like an obvious place for a political history to start, so why is this the first book to do it? Why do histories of Britain so often tend to focus instead on national institutions and identity? An element of the answer is itself the effect of a kind of path dependency (some other elements of the answer are considered in the Conclusion). History emerged as a professional discipline in the late nineteenth century when European nation states were proving to be the most powerful political organizations on the planet. Not surprisingly, many historians and other social scientists were very interested in the origins of those states and since the UK was the most powerful of those states, understanding its development seemed to be particularly important for understanding the modern world.

These remain valid interests, of course, but we now face other, more pressing questions. Globalization and the rise of much larger nation states have cut European states down to size, and made other political questions seem more important. Nonetheless, a preoccupation with understanding the evolution of British political institutions is still imprinted on our public history like the Cheshire cat's grin.

Changing the starting point leads to some radical shifts in perspective. Most fundamentally, it connects the history of life on Britain with much larger regions, effectively globalizing our view, and this is clearly a useful perspective given current political concerns. From the Neolithic period onwards the record of collective action on Britain reveals a history connected to or parallel with a much broader history of humanity, and over the long run the geography of culture and power has not mapped on to the island very neatly at all. Only in the recent past has it (along with part of the neighbouring one) been politically united and its inhabitants thought of themselves as British, and there is much more to be learned from its political history than how that came about. People have got things done by organizing at larger and smaller scales throughout the period covered by this book, which (as we have seen) is really the whole period in which we can say anything much about collective action.

Seeing British history this way goes against a deep-rooted tradition of telling some version of 'our island story'. Formally speaking, the island is Great Britain and the state is the United Kingdom (of Great Britain and Northern Ireland), but the two are routinely conflated, as in the recurring political promise to make Britain (that is, the UK) 'great again'. However, as we will see, the conflation is not as self-evidently natural as generations of Britons have been taught to assume. Nor is it a general rule that islands are self-contained political entities: in fact, they hardly ever are. If Greenland is the largest thing we can refer to as an island, then Great Britain is the ninth largest (ranked by surface area). Of the top ten only Madagascar is both an island and an independent state. Indeed, of the top fifty only another four are self-contained states—Iceland, Cuba, Sri Lanka, and Taiwan. The others are divided (like New Guinea or Borneo) or parts of a larger political entity (like Greenland, Sumatra, Honshu, and, indeed, Great Britain).[1] Of course, the issue is more complicated than this, but at the very least this suggests that we should hesitate to think of islands as *naturally* self-contained political communities. Dropping this assumption makes this book quite consciously a history centred on a geographical region (Great Britain) rather than on the story of a political community (the UK)—it is a history of political life *on* Britain rather than *in* Britain.

The history of collective life on Britain has always been connected with that elsewhere, but it is also, of course, unique. Like every other geographical region, Great Britain's political experience has been particular to that place, and path dependency is important to understanding that uniqueness. However, to explain patterns of political life on Great Britain it is almost always necessary to understand a larger context, and to see how those wider developments impacted differently on different parts of the island. In one sense it is a variety of global history—how did this region share in wider developments, and how does its experience parallel that of other regions? That helps sharpen our sense of what is particular about the current phase of globalization. There have been many other points when the political life of Great Britain has been connected to a much wider portion of the globe: that is not what is new about the current context.

Above all, opening up past experience in this way helps us to think about one of the most pressing questions in contemporary life—how to act together to achieve the things that we need to do. In talking about this I use the term 'agency', meaning by that the capacity to exert an influence over our social and material world. That is a restricted sense of the term—it does not, for example, imply full autonomy or the capacity to achieve full flourishing, but simply the capacity to act together to influence the conditions in which individuals and groups make their lives. It is this kind of agency that Karl Marx had in mind when he wrote that 'Men make their own history, but they do not make it just as they please; they do not make it under circumstances chosen by themselves, but under circumstances directly encountered, given and transmitted from the past.'[2] The book is both about those conditions as they were encountered and about what people were able to do about them.

In that sense this is a history for use. De-centring Westminster by making the history of Britain about something much broader reflects an important current in contemporary politics. Westminster politicians are no longer regarded as people who can command events. Young idealists in the twentieth century often thought about how control of national governments could deliver a new and perfected society. Young idealists in the twenty-first century think more often about how international solidarities and movements are essential to achieving meaningful change. Many other voters have a deep suspicion of national politicians after years of being over-promised. In that context, a history of people, power, and agency is more useful in understanding the present and thinking about the future than a history of the origins of Westminster government and British identity.

*   *   *

The book is divided into eight chapters. The first four flesh out and illustrate these general arguments about how political power works. Chapter 1 illustrates in more detail how much of the history of political life can be understood as a dialogue between collective power over the social and material world and the differential power of one person or group over others. It gives examples of how this relationship has been formalized in legal and institutional arrangements and how that both creates possibilities and sets limits for the future. People address challenges using the collective institutions they have inherited. They are empowered or limited by that institutional inheritance and by how successfully they can modify it for immediate purposes—this is the path dependency that often distinguishes one political society from another.

Three thematic chapters then explore the factors which shape how collective institutions are used: mobilizing ideas, the material conditions people encounter, and their collective organizational capacity. How we understand the world defines what needs to be done and how to do it; over time, changes in dominant ideas have led to dramatic changes in how political power has been used. Similarly, political power is often used to deal with real, material challenges—as in the present, for example, with the great fluidity of global capital or the threat of climate change and global pandemic. What is done also depends on available institutions. Organizational and technological capacity set limits on what is achievable, but also create new possibilities for action—for example, the potentially huge changes in how societies are policed made possible by the digital revolution and Big Data analysis.

The second half of the book explores changing patterns in the use of collective institutions. Chapter 5 looks at the geographies of power, illustrating that getting things done has not always or naturally led people to act as Britons, but also at smaller and larger scales too: manor, parish, lordship, town, and county, or through interstate and transnational organizations. Chapter 6 outlines who has had the power to affect what collective institutions have been used for at these various scales of action, and how they achieved it. What (if anything) have those with less differential power, or those largely excluded from it, been able to do to shape how collective institutions have been used? These lead, in Chapter 7, to an outline of the history of political life on Great Britain over the long run. It is organized around phases in the history of political power defined by broad shifts in ideas, material conditions, and organizational forms. The main landmarks in this narrative are not new, but the perspective from which we see them is.

The Conclusion draws out two key themes of the book: how this changes our view of the relationship between the history of Britain and a wider global history; and, secondly, how thinking about agency offers a 'history for use' when reflecting on our own political situation. We can think of that first shift as a change from understanding how Britain, through industrialization, democratization, and empire, made the modern world to an understanding of how, over the much longer term, the world made modern Britain. The aim is to find a more useful way to think about political life over the long run, one which makes our understanding of past experience more relevant to current political debates.

1

POLITICAL LIFE

Power Over Our World, Power Over Each Other

The various phases of construction at Stonehenge must have relied on someone or some people having the power to demand and direct labour. As we have seen, this is the difference between *collective power* (the power we exercise together over our social and material world) and *differential power* (the power of one person or group over others, power which is distributed unevenly across society).

These forms of power are in continual dialogue. Collective power is not necessarily mobilized voluntarily, and it is likely that people will want to set limits on the differential power of those coordinating collective action, perhaps in an explicit legal arrangement or the creation of an institution regulated by clear rules. This is the role of *institutionalization*. For example, draining a marsh might require giving a coordinating group differential power to direct the labour and make decisions relating to the land of other people. The result is a collective power to drain the marsh, but a differential power for those organizing the work. In order to regulate that power a drainage committee might be established. This institution tries to achieve something for the community that the individuals could not achieve for themselves—exercising a collective power. But it also regulates that differential power, giving assurance that the committee's decisions are properly restrained and appropriately directed. In other words, collective power is both a capacity to get things done, and a way to restrain differential power. The relationship between the two is formalized in *collective institutions* or perhaps regulated by law. This is the function of public law (which regulates the powers of government) and an independent judiciary.

Collective institutions act at the direction and command of individuals or groups who, as a result, have differential power. There is therefore a risk that they come to serve the interests of those who control them or become a means to entrench elite privilege. This is true at large scales—supranational organizations and nation states—and at more local scales—drainage committees, town and parish councils, and so on. Institutions of all kinds can be seen in that sense as formalizing power relations. But it is not usually a once-and-for-all agreement. Over time collective institutions are subject to pressure to ensure that they continue to serve genuinely collective ends rather than, for example, particular vested interests.

Another important feature of collective institutions is that they create path dependencies. People acting in the present often use the tools they have to hand, including their institutional inheritance. So, the draining of the marsh might create other problems of environmental or economic organization—issues relating to water supply, the division of common land, or forms of sustainable agriculture, for example—and the committee might offer a convenient tool with which to address them. The way that those challenges are addressed in our village might therefore differ from a neighbouring village that had never established a drainage committee. Eventually the drainage committee might do all sorts of things which are also done elsewhere, but not by a drainage committee: a path dependency is created which means similar problems are addressed differently according to the local institutional inheritance.

The evolution of the English parliament gives a real-world illustration of path dependency. It was originally a body convened at the monarch's pleasure to advise him or her, and gradually acquired rights and powers in relation to the advice, legislation, and money that it delivered for the monarch. Over time it became the seat of executive authority and a representative (in theory at least) of all the citizens of the UK, something quite different from the institution as it was first created. This happened by gradual evolution: as it proved useful for one purpose, a new capacity was created, and that potential was used for the future. Magna Carta would be an equally resonant English example—initially a deal between the king and his barons to solve an immediate impasse, it made more general claims that have been interpreted more and more broadly over time.

Much of political life can be understood in this way, as a dialogue between collective and differential power, the institutionalization and regulation of both, and the path dependencies it creates which distinguish one political system from another.

This chapter illustrates these relationships through the example of the growth of the Roman empire, then discusses the issues through two thematic examples—the history of taxation and public works, both of which involve a negotiation of the relationship between support for collective action (the 'public good') and the protection of private property rights. Finally, it briefly discusses British views of the EU from this perspective, of the regulation of the differential power of those coordinating the use of collective institutions.

The Roman Empire: Collective Institutions and Differential Power

A betting person would not, in 1000 BCE, have backed the inhabitants of Rome to dominate Great Britain. That is the date of the earliest evidence of permanent settlement in Rome, and 200 years later there were reed and clay huts on the Palatine Hill. These were the characteristic dwellings of a population that lived by subsistence farming. By the early sixth century there are signs of a wall but little to suggest the capacity for collective action demonstrated at Stonehenge 1,500 years earlier.

However, within a relatively short space of time Rome became the centre of one of the great Iron Age empires, developing sophisticated collective institutions and leaving a very full record of the ideas that drove its development, as well as an archaeological record of its impact on the social and material environment of north-west Europe far more dramatic than anything that had come before. The standard accounts of this illustrate the trade-offs between collective and differential power.

Rome was originally a monarchy, evolving into a Republic as institutions were built which mobilized collective power more effectively. It was later said, for example, that under the last Roman Kings, the city had been organized into '*centuries*'. Each provided soldiers and was represented for legislative, electoral, and judicial purposes in the *comitia centuriata*, the Centuriate Assembly. The *centuries* were organized according to wealth, so that overall there was a clear idea of who could supply what to the army, but also a limit on that: a collective capacity that was also regulated by collective agreement. Collective institutions had been used to restrain rather than to protect the differential power of elites, regulating who did what to support those institutions and who got what benefits as a result, and making them at the same time more effective.

By that time Rome had absorbed the territory of the Etruscans, a significant military power to the north which had previously been far more significant than Rome. Etruscan power had declined under pressure from its rivals, and the Romans had been able to absorb the heartland, offering security to Etruscan elites in return for their cooperation. The power of Roman collective institutions in this case may have *served* elite interests: Etruscan elites may have submitted to Roman authority in order to shore up their privilege.

Although the creation of more effective collective institutions had depended on broader social integration in Rome, those collective institutions may then have become a way of entrenching particular interests such as those of the Etruscan elites. Certainly, this dynamic explains much of the story of the rise of Rome—increasingly efficient military organization led to conquest and the expansion of trade; but also entrenched vested interests, encouraged corruption, and threatened a tyranny by those in charge. As well as channelling greater wealth into the empire, military success bred wealth and power for civilian elites and military commanders.

As a result, there were attempts to re-balance this relationship to give greater benefits to the populace at large—for example, in the reforms proposed by the Gracchus brothers, Tiberius and Gaius, between 133 and 121 BCE. Land seized by conquest, or forfeit to Rome, became 'public land'. Tiberius proposed that no single individual could hold more than around 300 acres of public land (with extra allowed for sons), allowing the rest of it to be used to help the landless. It was in effect an attempt to prevent a land grab by those in power, and to ensure the benefits of Roman conquest were distributed more widely among those who contributed to it. This direct challenge to vested interests resulted in a battle for office and influence as Tiberius tried to get into a position to push through these measures. It ended in his violent murder. His brother Gaius then took up the cause of reform, continuing to propose redistributive policies, to extend rights of citizenship, and to ensure supplies of grain at reasonable prices to the Roman population. There was a further battle for office, to influence elections and to increase the powers of those offices most likely to support reform and so on. Once again, though, it ended in violent death, this time not just of the leader, Gaius, but of 3,000 of his supporters.

As in Rome's earliest days, when Etruscan elites seem to have embraced Roman authority to secure their own position, its collective institutions could be made to support vested interests and entrench elite power. Some individuals and groups profited disproportionately, even corruptly, from their military effectiveness. Equally, though, as in the days of the last kings, the Gracchus brothers attempted to use the collective power of the population to restrain the differential power of military and political elites, and to use collective institutions to deliver wider benefits.[1]

In subsequent centuries those who saw the Roman frontier advancing towards them faced similar choices. Julius Caesar led expeditions to Britain in 55 and 54 BCE. His own motivation reflected the dynamics of Roman political life—building up his power through conquest and the spoils of victory—and by the lure of Britain's precious metals. The pretext, though, was the flight of Mandobrocius, the son of a king based in East Anglia, killed by Cassivellaunus, leader of the tribes based north of the Thames centred in what is now Hertfordshire. Roman power was a resource for Mandobrocius, making it worth submitting to the personal power of Caesar.

Although Caesar's expeditions came to nothing, in the following century British elites showed signs of engaging with Roman life voluntarily, adapting Roman manners and style. British coins included Latin inscriptions and bore images that reflected Roman rather than British artistic taste, while elite grave goods and hoards of precious objects included Roman objects, coins, and even a helmet.[2] But to gain access to Roman power local elites had to acknowledge the power that men like Caesar now had over them.

After the concerted Claudian conquest in 43, the Roman province took shape as an amalgam of client kingdoms and areas transformed into Roman patterns of administration. Some local rulers, such as Cogidubnus, were able to build up their power with Roman backing and it may have been Cogidubnus who lived in splendour at Fishbourne. The magnificent villa there was built on a massive scale only thirty years after the invasion, on the site of an invasion-period military base. Built in the latest style, with imported marble and magnificent mosaics and furnished with fashionable objects, it would have been instantly recognizable to a visitor from Rome as the house of someone fully connected with contemporary Roman culture. If it was the house of Cogidubnus it is hard to imagine a clearer demonstration of the benefits of cooperating with Roman power.[3] For others, though, the demands of the Romans seemed unbearable and some Britons who had initially cooperated later rebelled. Accepting the benefits of Roman rule—the massively superior power of its collective institutions—also entailed the acceptance of the differential power of Rome's military men and administrators. Failure to accept that led usually to disaster.

A kind of equilibrium was reached before the whole island was absorbed, though. Raids on the prosperity of Romanized Britain, or the threat of them, drew the army into expansion, as did the internal dynamics of Roman politics. But the threat to the stability of the empire posed by successful warlords drew the Emperor Hadrian into a programme of consolidation. A line was drawn and a stable limit set—one of the most visible marks of Roman collective power on the island, Hadrian's Wall. It probably took 15,000 men about six years to build it—not just a huge wall and ditch stretching for 73 miles, but milecastles, towers, turrets, and forts, as well as large civil settlements such as those at Vindolanda and Housesteads. Here perhaps is the most startling demonstration of the political change—a stone structure on a scale vastly greater than could have been achieved by earlier generations on the island—far greater of course than Stonehenge—and something not rivalled for centuries afterwards (Figure 1).

The wall may not have been a defensive structure but rather a means to monitor movement in and out of the province (most of the troops were positioned well south of it). What is clear, though, is that inside the limit that it symbolized were those who enjoyed the benefits of the *Pax Romana* (Roman peace)—not least the defence of their lives and livelihood. But the collective institutions of the Roman system also generated enormous differential power. Within the empire this led to battles for control of tribute

Figure 1. Hadrian's Wall

and taxation, and scenes of Gothic horror expressing the power of some individuals over others. On Great Britain, though, the trade-off between the benefits of rule by Rome's collective institutions and the resultant differential power of those who controlled them seems to have proved largely stable. What fatally unbalanced Roman rule on Britain was not internal contests for power or revolts against the Roman order, such as that led by Boudicca and later rebels; it was external shocks, the weaknesses of the Roman centre, and the attractiveness of Britain as a base from which to compete for imperial power which ended Roman rule on the island.

Private Property and the Public Good

Much of the history of political life on Britain can be understood in this way, as the interplay of collective and differential power:

not just the rise and expansion of the Roman empire, but also the formation of the Anglo-Saxon kingdoms and the regulation of relationships between king and subjects, the rise of parliamentary government, or the debate about the relationship with the EU. Each of these collective institutions delivers power over the social and material world in return for acceptance of the differential power of those coordinating political action. That differential power is in turn regulated in forms of agreement with those subject to government.

It is equally easy to illustrate the benefits of collective power: in the relatively recent past the lives saved by the Clean Air Act (1956) and its successors, or the measures in the 1960s including the Road Safety Act (1967) which tightened up the drink-driving laws and required new cars to have seat belts. There were clear benefits to health and housing from the creation of the NHS or the Town and Country Planning Act (1947); to the low paid from the introduction of the minimum wage (1999) and to the whole population from the decisive and successful intervention of the UK government in the aftermath of the 2008 financial crash.[4]

Rather than try to explore this relationship comprehensively, however, I take here a single thematic example over the long run: the relationship between private property and the public good; that is, between individual property rights and collective power.

During the ninth and tenth centuries the kingdoms of lowland Britain were threatened with extinction by Viking raids and settlement. A critically important response in the Anglo-Saxon part of Great Britain was the agreement to raise money to make an annual payment to the Danes in return for guaranteed peace, starting in 991. This had huge effects on Anglo-Saxon society, involving the creation of a system to allocate the burden which seems to have led, within a couple of decades, to a dramatic transfer of wealth to the Vikings—Scandinavian hoards from this period contain large quantities of Anglo-Saxon coins.[5] This was a significant exercise of collective power—allowing Anglo-Saxons to act together to take control over the circumstances of their lives.

This was done according to set rules—how much was due from what kind of land and so on, and how the money was to be used. The power of the collective was mobilized, creating differential power for the king; and that differential power was regulated. This regulation was probably not achieved by negotiation, although the precise detail of the original arrangements is obscure. Nonetheless it does seem that some elite figures reached formal and lasting agreements about what they should contribute, and on what basis that would be calculated. The formal requirement to gain consent for taxation was a much later achievement, probably of the thirteenth century, but the Danegeld (as it was later to be known) had been institutionalized—it evolved into a regular form of collective action, with recognized powers and limits, which allowed for predictable, limited, and to some degree legitimate action.[6] This land tax was retained after the Norman Conquest and used for different purposes—it was for a while in fact more or less unique in western Europe.[7] It had created a capacity which English kings used for the future, and the way it was regulated shaped how future kings could or could not try to do similar things.

For example, in the 1630s the English King Charles I wanted to update his navy, but without using parliament to raise money. The design of merchant and military vessels was gradually diverging so that monarchs increasingly needed specialized fighting ships and could no longer simply borrow merchant ships and fit them for war. Previous monarchs had established a right to demand that their subjects should provide ships, but as the demands of war changed this gradually shifted to providing the money for the king to acquire the right kind of ship. From 1635 onwards Charles pushed this right to raise ship money, claiming that there was a national emergency affecting the whole kingdom, and that he could therefore ask everyone in the kingdom to provide money to acquire the necessary ships. The cost was parcelled out to each county and county governors asked to raise the relevant portion from the inhabitants. There was a complex legal hearing about this—whether people were obliged to believe the king when he said there was an emergency; if they were, whether they had to pay up or if they could wait for a parliament to give the king the money he needed; and if people refused, whether this could be enforced as a debt to the king (the counter-case being that since they were being asked for a bit of a ship due from the county, they owed the rest of the county a bit of a ship, rather than the king some money). The principles are clear—the need for collective defence, rights in private property, and the detailed regulation of the relationship between the two—but the form of the discussion is highly technical and, frankly, odd. These strange and convoluted legal arguments are an example of how previous decisions and settlements set the terms for future argument. Among the numerous precedents cited to decide whether or not Ship Money was legal was the Danegeld, first raised more than 650 years previously.[8]

Moreover, the measures taken in the seventeenth century were themselves important for subsequent generations, and Ship Money, for example, became a precedent. The judgment was cited in a landmark constitutional case 400 years later about commandeering private property during the First World War. In

1916 De Keyser's Royal Hotel, which had not been thriving, was requisitioned for use by the Royal Flying Corps and after the war the owner claimed compensation. The requisition depended on the 'prerogative power' of the sovereign which, in effect, over-rode the normal property rights of the citizen. Such prerogative powers originally belonged to the monarch independently of parliament but are now exercised in the name of the monarch, usually by the prime minister. While it is clear that new prerogative powers cannot be created, it is equally clear that prerogative powers do not depend on parliamentary sanction.

In this particular case, the legal argument concentrated on whether private property could be requisitioned by prerogative power without compensation. The judges ruled that the prerogative is in abeyance when statute law can be found to provide assistance to the complainant: in other words, that the statute does not abolish the prerogative, but in particular cases it can mean that a prerogative power does not apply. They neither denied the essential prerogative power to requisition nor asserted that statute law trumped the prerogative in general. Instead, they ruled that the owner of the hotel was entitled to compensation under the 1842 Defence Act: the existence of a relevant statute offering protection to the citizen meant that the prerogative power to seize property without compensation was in abeyance.[9] They had not challenged the power of senior military commanders to decide what was necessary for national defence—such a judgement was not a matter for the judges. It was on this point that they cited Ship Money: that the court could not second guess the King's judgement. It is hard to make sense of this set of arguments without understanding the long prior history of the relationship between collective institutions and private property and how that had been institutionalized in the UK.

This is one form of path dependency: that the institutionalization of power frames future discussions about how it can be
used. Another is that once a collective institution is established it
can be used for all sorts of other purposes. The basic unit of taxation for the Danegeld was the 'hide', which could be used to raise
money for all sorts of things: local rates for the maintenance of
highways and bridges, and the militia might all use arrangements
worked out for national taxation. The opposite was also true—
that demands from the Crown were parcelled out according to
local arrangements made for other purposes. By the later sixteenth century, for example, regular rates were being imposed in
many parts of England to deal with poverty—to house, employ,
feed, or punish the poor—and these had a complicated relationship to rating and administrative systems for national taxation.

Taxation also has significant uses beyond simply spending and
borrowing: powers to tax and spend have become a means for governments to manage individual behaviour and the economy as a
whole. Within a few years of the Ship Money controversy Charles
I's government had broken down (for reasons much broader and
more complex than Ship Money). In winning the subsequent civil
war parliament created new forms of taxation which transformed
the state: powers created to win the civil war were retained
by the restored monarchy and helped lay the foundations of
the UK's great power status (see Chapter 6). An unintended
consequence of this was that the government became the biggest
spender in the economy, and thereafter its fiscal (tax and spending)
policies were used increasingly consciously not just to raise
money but also to shape economic activity. Fiscal policy can be
used to raise relative prices—such as by making imported cars
more expensive than ones produced at home in order to protect

jobs. This can be done to incentivize changes in individual behaviour too—to stop smoking or drinking, to use hybrid cars, to install solar panels, and so on. That governments have this power is not a reflection of the initial intentions behind the Danegeld, but a product of the long history of using an established power or institution to deal with a new problem or opportunity.

Each of these examples is more complicated than I have set them out here, but all of them represent the negotiation of powers to tax—the balance between, on the one hand, the collective power delivered by taxation and the benefits that can be claimed for it and, on the other, the restraint of governments and protection of individual property. And each resolution frames future discussion and the potential for future action—one example of the path dependency which makes political entities different from one another.

Public Works

Public works have raised similar issues. For example, for centuries London has faced environmental problems resulting from population growth and high population density. In 1520 it probably had 60,000 inhabitants, about five times as many as Norwich, which was then the second largest city on Great Britain. By 1700 London had grown nearly ten times bigger—575,000—and was nineteen times the size of Norwich. During the eighteenth century it continued to grow rapidly and at a rate that far outstripped its provincial rivals, reaching a million sometime soon after 1800. This growth was only possible because of in-migration since the death rate in London was higher than the birth rate.[10] This rapid growth, fuelled by constant migration, fed a city in which there was no single coordinating authority—what we think of as London was divided administratively between the cities of London and Westminster and spread beyond both of them into Southwark south of the river and to areas to the north and east.

This created problems which prefigured those of the large industrial cities of the nineteenth century. One way of appreciating them is through the history of human waste—an unavoidable and largely private matter which had potentially catastrophic consequences for the collective good if not properly managed. In 1600 most houses in London had access to a privy, and some of them discharged directly into watercourses of the Thames. Many more, though, drained into a brick or stone-lined cess pool. These had to be dug out periodically—a truly unsavoury and not particularly safe task. It attracted a certain amount of dark humour at the expense of the men who did this work, known among other things as gong farmers, Tom Turdmen, or gold finders. The work itself was demanding. As described by Henry Mayhew in the nineteenth century, tubs were dipped into the cess pool until they could not reach the ordure, at which point 'holemen' went down on ladders and shovelled the waste directly into the tubs, each of which might weigh over 50kg when full. The tubs were raised by ropemen and carried by tubmen to a waiting cart, into which they were emptied from the tops of ladders.[11] It was heavy and deeply unpleasant work: once disturbed the stench from cess pits could be unbearable, and to protect the public at large this work had to be conducted after 9 pm. There were also tight controls over where the 'night soil men' could dump the ordure they had dug.

These private initiatives were insufficient to cope with further spectacular growth in population of the city in the first half of the nineteenth century, when London's population grew from around

1 million to nearly 2.4 million. Arrangements for sanitation were no different in the early nineteenth century from those of the fifteenth. At that point 200,000 houses had cess pools beneath them, and effluent was sometimes forced upwards through the wooden floorboards of poorer households. The growing popularity of water closets increased the demand for water at the same time that the population was rocketing, and many of the water closets drained into the watercourses from which drinking water was drawn.[12]

In 1838 a report by Edwin Chadwick attributed an outbreak of typhus to sewerage problems. However, management of water and sewerage in London was divided between seven Crown-appointed commissioners. Chadwick's proposal for a single commission with responsibility for the whole of London met determined opposition from existing authorities, and his ideas were not implemented. The collective institution established to tackle the issue would have created a differential power in the hands of that body that others found unacceptable.

Three cholera outbreaks between 1848 and 1854 carried off tens of thousands of victims, but by then the idea of a single commission had been abandoned. However, in that part of the conurbation governed by the Corporation of the City of London the death rate had been low. This seemed to be a result of the enforced cleaning of privies, emptying of cess pits, removal of ordure, and the regular inspection of lodging houses. Using its own powers, the Corporation had apparently dramatically limited the impact of cholera—of the 10,000 deaths in the 1854 cholera outbreak only 200 were within its jurisdiction.

This public health success by a subordinate jurisdiction meant that the decentralizers won: the differential power of the central body was strictly regulated. In 1855 a Metropolitan Board of Works was created but it really only oversaw a system comprising thirty-eight small bodies. Each of these bodies chose three representatives for the Board, which never achieved the status enjoyed, for example, by the Corporation of London. It could not appoint its own medical officer, nor could it force vestries (responsible for individual parishes) and district boards (responsible for larger areas) to meet their obligations. Handicapped by these restrictions, it had achieved little in its first three years but in 1858 a hot summer encouraged the 'Great Stink' and the Metropolitan Board of Works was finally able to implement a major sewer project. An east–west sewer was constructed, intercepting the ancient sewers and discharging in the Thames far down stream of the main built-up area (Figure 2).[13]

Attempts to establish a single authority to deal with the sanitation problem in the capital had been hampered by concern at the differential power it would have. This delayed the work, and in fact eventually discredited the Metropolitan Board of Works, which was brought down amid accusations of back-scratching and corruption in its contracting. Nonetheless, the success of the public health measures taken in London should not be underestimated—over the later nineteenth century the annual death rate dropped from twenty-five per 1,000 to fifteen—and the Metropolitan Board of Works deserves some of the credit for that.

Other nineteenth-century city authorities acted in similar ways, and arguably to more effect. Joseph Chamberlain led a programme of urban improvement in Birmingham that fostered enormous civic pride. As Mayor during the 1870s he oversaw the purchase of two private gas companies, eliminating disruptive rival infrastructure projects, and turning a significant profit for the city. The

Figure 2. The Prince of Wales at the opening of the main drainage works at Crossness, 1865

water supply was also taken over from private enterprise and an ambitious slum clearance project was launched which dramatically reduced death rates. Chamberlain encouraged local pride in civic educational and cultural institutions and his programme of 'municipal socialism' was widely admired around the globe.[14]

Nevertheless, a tension between public works and private rights has been a recurring feature of political life. For example, compulsory purchase orders have been used throughout the post-war period to remove private obstructions to the achievement of such public purposes. They allow local and national authorities to acquire land and property without consent (but with compensation) and have been essential to the achievement of large infrastructure projects such as motorway or railway building. They have been used by local authorities when developing town centres too. In essence, they allow the public good—defined by local authorities—to trump individual property rights. They reflect an ambition to plan the economy and urban environment that can be traced back to the nineteenth century, extended in such social experiments as the building of 'garden cities' after 1898. The planning system has been elaborated to give individuals and groups the opportunity to negotiate these same interests, between public and private projects on one hand and individuals' own property rights and amenities on the other.

This is one way of thinking about the nationalization of private industries too—which is done with compulsion and compensation. After the Second World War a massive programme of nationalization was undertaken this way, driven by a desire to be able to manage the economy (particularly with a view to maximizing employment), to balance the private and public sectors, and to take control of strategic industries or services thought to be natural monopolies. Nationalization, in effect, takes over private interests and profits in order to serve a vision of the collective interest. An ambitious programme of nationalization in the late 1940s began with the Bank of England and the coal industry, followed by the transport sector, then gas and electricity, and in the early 1950s by iron and steel. At that point 10 per cent of the population was employed in nationalized industries. It had all been made possible by legislation and compensation (to the tune of £2.6 bn). Opposition to nationalization has not usually challenged this principle that compulsory purchase with compensation can be imposed for the public good; instead argument has usually been about the efficiency or effectiveness of nationalized industries in delivering the promised collective benefit.[15]

Collective and Differential Power: The EU

These examples of the balance between collective and differential power could be multiplied more or less indefinitely and not just around the issue of governments, taxation, and private property. For example, governments have over time acquired and lost the power to conscript men for military service—to demand potentially life-threatening service from an individual in the name of the collective good. Other projects for collective security have raised significant worries about individual liberty—most recently, for example, in the relationship between the powers of intelligence services or law enforcement agencies to monitor communication, and rights to privacy. The potential to improve our collective security is balanced against the power it gives those agencies to know more about us than we do about them. That differential power is in turn limited by agreements about the conditions under which it can be used—avoiding, if possible, a 'snoopers' charter'.

The balance of collective and differential power goes to the heart of British concerns about the European Union and was a critical issue in the referendum debate in 2016. As we will see in Chapter 3, in the aftermath of the Second World War it became clear that some political challenges required collective action at increasing scale—peace, security, and management of the global economy, for example. In fact, one of the early steps in the creation of what has become the EU was coordination of some of the key industries that were being nationalized in the UK—coal and steel. Since that time inter-governmental agencies have proliferated all around the globe—defence and security pacts, free trade areas and customs unions, as well as institutions for global economic and security management such as the UN, the IMF, and the World Bank. On the whole the collective capacity created in these agencies arose from the cooperation of national states. The power to do things still depends on securing the cooperation of nation states and, like the London Metropolitan Board of Works, the capacity of the overarching coordinating body is limited but not negligible.

The EU stands out among many of these forms of inter-governmental cooperation in having a more ambitious aim—to act not simply as an inter-governmental body, but as a supranational one. This delivers, potentially, a much greater collective capacity, as yet mainly explored in economic matters relating to the creation of a single market. It also has much greater differential power in relation to national governments. The EU is something of a hybrid, therefore, consisting both of inter-governmental bodies (like the Council of Ministers) and supranational bodies (like the Commission and the Parliament). A key change in the balance of these elements can be made in apparently technical changes such as the change from the need for unanimity in the Council of Ministers to qualified majority voting. This has meant that an individual government cannot simply block a measure that is against the minister's view of the national interest.

To opponents of the EU these supranational elements are a threat to national sovereignty and hence to national self-determination, and the failure of successive UK governments to prevent developments in this direction was a key reason many wanted to leave the

EU. For others the balance of the advantages of access to the collective power of the EU against the ceding of differential power to its key institutions seemed less alarming, a matter of 'trade-offs'—surrendering a degree of control over some political functions in return for more effective collective capacity, at a larger scale, in others. What has not happened, so far, is the collective power of the supranational institutions of the EU being subjected to effective restraint by the European population at large. There is a widespread concern that there is no coherent European electorate exerting pressure on its MEPs, and that no effective pressure can be applied by the European people on the actions of the EU except via their national governments.

*　*　*

In one sense, then, this aspect of the Brexit debate is the stuff of conventional political and constitutional history—the history of collective institutions, their powers and restraint of those powers, institutional inheritance and path dependency. The same issues can be seen at work in the politics of the rise of Rome and the long constitutional histories of the Kingdoms of England and Scotland, as well as of the UK. These same distinctions also offer a way to understand the development of institutions below the national level, such as the government of the rapidly industrializing cities of the nineteenth century.

The critical points for the argument of this book concern:

- the distinction between collective and differential political power and how the relationship between these two things is a central dynamic of political life;

- how these relationships are regulated by institutions, which embody rules and constitutions to frame them (so that we can in fact think of collective institutions as ways of regularizing power relations);
- how such institutions create possibilities but also limits on future action (path dependency).

Because these relationships operate above and below the level of the nation, we cut ourselves off from a wide range of historical experience of using collecting power if we concentrate too closely on the origins of Westminster government and its associated political identity—Britishness.

2

MOBILIZING IDEAS AND THE USES OF COLLECTIVE INSTITUTIONS

Ideas fundamentally shape how collective institutions work and how they are used. Different societies with the same economic and political capacity will act differently because they believe different things. We have seen this already—that late Neolithic people on Britain built circular ditches and banks which often enclosed stone circles, while their contemporaries across the rest of Europe did not. In the Cold War period some states invested heavily in athletic performance, in pursuit of what might now be called soft power and a positive brand; others did not. Ideas also set limits on the differential power of those in control of collective institutions—for example, those of Christian rulership or the democratic mandate offer resources for different interest groups to try to influence how those institutions actually work.

This chapter illustrates how the spread of new ideas has offered new ways to think about the workings of collective institutions and shaped their use. These issues are illustrated by examples arranged in roughly chronological order, but (of course) this is not a full history of the influence of ideas on politics. Instead it illustrates, firstly, how ideas have shaped power *relations*, through the example of the 'feudal compact'. The second section of the chapter looks at how ideas have shaped the *uses* of collective institutions—defining the challenges that need to be addressed and appropriate responses. It uses the example of the impact of Roman and Christian ideas on Anglo-Saxon kingship and then the importance of a quantifying impulse in recent centuries: the influence of statistical and probabilistic thinking on what became political economy. The third section illustrates how powerful ideas have driven political conflict and resistance—a tension between Church and state, or religion and politics, and the role of diverse and contested ideas in affecting power relations.

The key point is that ideas have an independent effect on collective life. Powerful people do not control them or how they are understood and appealing to them can have unintended and unexpected consequences. Their geography has never matched that of the institutions through which people act. As a consequence, these institutions have a parallel history with those elsewhere acting under the influence of the same ideas, but more than that, they share a history as they respond at the same time to the same ideas and what they demand from us. The life of collective institutions cannot be understood without understanding the key ideas that give them life and legitimacy.

Ideas and Power Relations

Inheritance, Tenure, and the 'Feudal Compact'

Following the end of Roman rule the territory of what is now England was splintered, while in Scotland and Wales authority was divided among a number of competing powers. Two key ideas—inheritance and the feudal compact—were critical in the subsequent development and consolidation of larger kingdoms from these smaller entities. Both established stability of authority and property ownership through time, fundamentally shaping how power was regulated and used. This helped to stabilize these kingdoms, and they eventually came to dominate Great Britain for around a thousand years, from their eighth-century origins (possibly earlier) until the nineteenth century (when the power of the monarchy became increasingly ceremonial and real authority came to rest in parliament).

In truth it is very hard to get an accurate picture of life on Britain after the collapse of Roman authority because the sources for political history are scant. However, what seems to have emerged was an island of tiny polities—perhaps ten or fifteen in the space now occupied by England—and the distinction between the Romanized part of the island and the rest was greatly diminished. In the south kings ruled with small warrior aristocracies, no longer raising public taxes as the Romans had done, but depending instead on more personal tribute from the lands they controlled.[1] It is often assumed that authority was exercised by warrior bands (or more pejoratively tribes): organized around loyalty to a charismatic warrior leader, commanding personal service in return for gifts as a reward for martial success. In this view followers were tied to their leader by personal loyalty rather than formal legal arrangements and leaders secured their position by their personal success and charisma.

In Scotland and Wales the end of Roman authority had a less dramatic effect. The archaeological evidence suggests that the influence of the Roman presence had been more limited—fewer

Roman objects appear among the survivals and there were no towns and little evidence, for example, of villas. Ptolemy, a Greek writer living under Roman authority in Alexandria, described the tribes in Scotland in the second century, but we have no real understanding of what the internal political life of those tribes was like. By the fourth century we hear of fewer tribes and in the period after Rome there are king lists for Scotland, and heroic poetry for Wales. The former suggests some stable recognition of overlordship, but how people succeeded to or held on to these titles is not clear, nor really is the relationship to territory or its inhabitants. The Welsh poetry reveals the values that bards celebrated in leaders—those of a warrior leader, who demonstrated their personal charisma and success through feasting and gift-giving—and that is suggestive about the nature of authority there.

One influential view of this is that elites outside the Romanized zone had been able to consolidate their power through control of Roman goods without ever being subject to Roman rule. Following the collapse of Roman authority they were able to sustain their position, which had always been largely independent of Rome, although interacting with it. Whereas the end of Roman rule in the south and east of the island led to collapse and political disintegration of structures dependent on Rome, in the less Romanized areas it was associated with consolidation and further integration.

Over the following centuries England saw the gradual development of a smaller number of more stable kingdoms under the authority of kings who inherited power, rather than winning it through military success. These hereditary monarchies were in place by the eighth century. In Scotland inheritance was determining succession by the ninth century, when Kenneth Mac Alpin achieved authority over the whole of the previously separate Pictish and Scottish kingdoms. By that time four relatively stable kingdoms had been established in Wales too—Gwynedd, Powys, Dyfed, and Deheubarth—and succession through the male line seems to have been an established—if not always observed—principle, and the territories over which sons ruled were not necessarily of the same extent as their fathers.

More stable succession was associated with more formal relations between rulers and their subjects—offering more than gifts and protection through more explicitly defined rights. At this time law codes in England and Wales are more clearly defined and recorded than previously, although it seems that there were strong continuities in their content, which might reflect a greater emphasis on the value of writing them down rather than a major change in thinking. Some land in England had been held by charter since the seventh century (bocland or bookland), and this had made it easier to buy and sell, while other land had been held by custom (folcland or folkland) which gave kin of the current owner much more control of its fate. So, the role of writing, title to land, and political relationships evolved in a complex way, and over a long period. If the chronology is not clear, however, the essential power of the ideas is: by the ninth century most of Great Britain was under a pattern of authority quite distinct from that of the Roman system on the one hand, but also increasingly distinct from that of the warrior leader on the other.

The adoption of the feudal compact from the late eleventh century onwards greatly strengthened these structures by giving ever clearer definition to relationships within these kingdoms and placing more and more weight on the written record. In essence a superior held the title to land, granting its use to an inferior in return for homage. These inferiors might then do the same with their inferiors—subinfeudation. This created quite clearly defined mutual responsibilities within a codified legal framework. Beyond that, historians differ in what they mean by the term 'feudalism': some use it to define a social system in a much broader sense. However, these basic formal and legal principles are often thought to characterize the kingdoms of the high middle ages—succession by inheritance and a monarchy that was both supported by and the guarantor of codified legal relationships among the inhabitants.

Feudalism in this formal and limited sense was brought to the island by the Normans. Their impact on England was part of a broader expansion that led to the establishment of kingdoms in Sicily and Southern Italy, as well as a prominent part in the Crusades. In England, though, the conquest was effected by the king himself, not by knights acknowledging fealty to him, and as a result the Norman system imposed in England was particularly thoroughgoing. In Scotland, by contrast, the spread of the feudal compact was the product of a more organic process as successive kings from David I (1124–53) onwards tried to establish their government through the aristocracy. In some areas of Scotland, at some moments, David and his successors drew explicitly on feudal models, but over time and in other regions, they worked in other ways to establish defined rights and obligations. It is more helpful to think of this as a process of the territorialization of aristocratic and royal authority—tying particular rights and obligations to particular territorial jurisdictions—rather than a coherent policy of anglicization or feudalization. The result was a more diverse pattern of elite power than in England. For example, the 'clans' were hybrids, based internally on kinship and other relationships tying subordinates to the chief, but often recognized with feudal titles granted by the Crown.[2] Wales also experienced feudalization in a more piecemeal way, the result of more gradual settlement than wholesale conquest. In both Scotland and Wales feudal law was combined with customary law in defining rights to land and succession, and the resolution of disputes. This was to have long-term consequences, affecting how inhabitants of the more fully formalized kingdom of England, and also lowlanders in Scotland, regarded their neighbours to the north and west.

These differing trajectories reflect variants on the reception of mobilizing ideas in structuring political life but demonstrate how profoundly ideas shape the structuring of power relations. Later mobilizing ideas such as nationalism, communism, and neoliberalism all have this quality, defining how political relationships should be structured but also what collective institutions should do.

Shaping the Uses of Collective Power

Roman Ideas and Their Legacy

There is some evidence in the archaeological record of the impact of changing ideas—notably in the changes that followed the arrival of the Beaker people about 2,500 years ago which signalled the end of megalith building and the related ritual landscapes. Instead, the visible changes in the landscape tended to be the construction of barrows that marked the lives of individuals or smaller groups, perhaps family lineages.[3] However, it becomes much easier to trace their impact after the arrival of the Romans. As a literate culture, or at least a literate culture whose writing survives, the Romans have left far more evidence of their lives than previous generations of inhabitants of Great Britain. From their writing we have, for the first time, direct access to some of the mobilizing ideas that animated a political system on Britain. In fact, what the Romans said to each other and what they thought about the world still helps to shape political life. Their legal thought is foundational for European law: the principles they worked out for dealing with all sorts of conflicts are often ones we still use. Similarly, their views about access to the law and what it means long outlasted their empire, as did the way they thought about republics, empires, the power of the people or of their governors, and how political decisions should be made.

While we know a lot about Roman life in general, there is less direct evidence about Roman Britain specifically than many people imagine. Nonetheless, we do have clear evidence of how Roman ideas shaped the lives of its inhabitants. There is a much-cited discussion of this from the Roman author Tacitus, describing how his father-in-law Agricola had encouraged the Britons to live 'in a peaceable and inactive manner by offering...the pleasures that would follow on such a way of living'. Agricola encouraged them to build temples, squares with public buildings, and private houses. Working privately and in public, he praised those who responded and criticized the laggards, fostering 'competition for public recognition [in] place of compulsion'. The children of leading Britons were educated in Roman ways, with the result that 'those who had once shunned the Latin language now sought fluency and eloquency in it'. Roman dress, including the toga, became fashionable and there was a 'slide toward the allurements of degeneracy'. This was less exciting than it sounds—assembly rooms, bathing establishments, and smart dinner parties—but to Tacitus it reflected a kind of colonization of the mind: 'the Britons called it civilization when it was really all part of their servitude'.[4] We have here a clear statement of the values and politics behind the Roman archaeological package—something we do not have for earlier ruptures in the archaeological record. For the first time we know the names of some ordinary people, and also something about how they presented themselves. DNA shows who was born a Briton by birth and who was not, but they are not otherwise distinguishable in the archaeological record; it also shows that the 'Romans' were very often not from Italy. Roman ideas, manners, and culture were clearly incredibly powerful.

Knowledge of Roman history and language still carries cultural prestige and we can see the mark of Roman ideas in the mottos of football clubs, hospitals, schools, and universities; in the architectural style of many of our public buildings; and in our collective institutions (more clearly in the US constitution perhaps, but there is a long legacy of 'Roman' political thought in Britain's collective institutions too).

After the end of Roman government in lowland Britain written sources become scarcer again, but the archaeological record can be made to speak about the beliefs of those societies. The immediate successors of the Romans certainly claimed some of their virtues and, although, for example, the Anglo-Saxons settled outside the walls of the Roman city of Londinium, they and their contemporaries across the Channel continued to appeal to images of Roman authority in projecting their own. When coins started to be produced in England again, apparently in seventh-century Kent, the iconography followed that of the Merovingians, across the Channel, which was ultimately of Roman origin.[5]

This emulation of Roman style might in fact be the explanation for Offa's Dyke, a major construction running north–south near the border between modern England and Wales. The Dyke is in many ways rather puzzling, and certainly hard to explain in simple functional terms. It consists of a ditch on the western ('Welsh') side and a bank on the eastern ('English') side. The ditch is on average about 7.6m wide and 1.4m deep, the bank on average about 10.4m wide and 1.8m high; it is probable that when first constructed the ditch was deeper, around 1.8m, and that the bank was a similar height. There is no evidence that the bank had any structure on the top, although there may have been. A modern and relatively conservative estimate is that it would have taken 675,000 working days to construct—that is, 10,000 men working at the same time could have completed it in a bit less than ten weeks. This was a major undertaking, although potentially achievable in a single working season, and must have been an important project for those who undertook it.

Why did they do it? This is difficult to answer, not least because we are not sure that it was really built during the reign of King Offa of Mercia (757–96)—that conventional wisdom really relies on a single piece of later text, although it is plausible that Offa had the capacity and motivation to do it. If we are only reasonably confident about that, it is even less easy to be sure why he wanted it done. It was built without gateways, so clearly as a barrier, but there is no evidence that it was itself a military platform or part of a broader system of defence like Hadrian's Wall. It helps define an important political boundary that was 149 miles long, but current expert opinion is that the Dyke itself was only 81 miles long: much of the boundary, in fact some of the parts most threatened by external powers, was not protected by the Dyke. It seems to have functioned without being manned, and the once popular view that behind the bank there had been a clear ride along which armed men could move freely appears to have no supporting evidence at all. From the western side it presented an obstacle at least 3.6m high from the bottom of the ditch to the top of the bank, and that would have prevented the easy movement of horses or livestock, although presenting a less significant barrier for armed men. If it was there to prevent cattle raids, however, it might have made sense to put the ditch on the other side, to present a greater obstacle to cattle being moved from east to west.

So, the question arises why so much effort would have been put into something with such limited defensive value. It may have been that it was a statement of power in the Roman style—important like other walls for what it said rather than what it did. Literary sources from this period seem to support the suggestion that digging ditches—undertaking massive earthworks—was associated with a demonstration of Mercian power, echoing Roman style and authority, again something observable in other parts of Europe between around 800 and the middle of the following century.[6]

Christianity and Anglo-Saxon Government

Roman values clearly persisted and helped to shape the Anglo-Saxon world view, but a more transformative belief for Anglo-Saxon kingship was probably Christianity. Of course, the two intertwined quite closely. There had been Christians in Roman Britain, perhaps in quite large numbers, and the religion persisted thereafter, particularly in Wales, but Christianity was revitalized and came to dominance through the work of missionaries. They came from Ireland and Rome from the later part of the sixth century onwards, and during the seventh century these rival forms had an uneasy relationship, famously, for example, in the arguments over the date of Easter. But the eventual triumph of largely Roman Christianity had a profound impact on Anglo-Saxon life. It played a key role in the development of Anglo-Saxon kingship towards the dynastic kingship of the high middle ages: it fundamentally shaped what monarchies were for.

The transformation can be pictured by comparing the image of kingship presented by the famous early seventh-century ship burial at Sutton Hoo, with the image, say, of King Edward the Confessor (1042–66) about 350 years later. The burial at Sutton includes a collection of grave goods similar to those in burials near Vendel in eastern Sweden. Quite what beliefs they express is not completely clear, but the material similarity indicates a strong connection between the world views of the communities that made these burials. However, it is possible that the person buried at Sutton Hoo is Raedwald, a man who exercised an overlordship over other kings in east Anglia. He was a convert to Christianity who was said to have maintained a pagan temple too, in deference to those in his court who were hostile to Christianity: a moment when a king looked both to Scandinavian tradition and the values of Roman Christianity.

It was also a moment when sharper differences were emerging between rulers and ruled. For example, Sutton Hoo was first used for relatively modest burials, but over time it became a more exclusively elite site apparently reflecting increased social differentiation. This also seems to have been true of some settlement sites during the eighth century. Anglo-Saxon kingship evolved alongside stronger status distinctions, and we might think of this as a natural process of social and political evolution.

Figure 3. The Sutton Hoo helmet

It was a complex process, therefore, but a key influence distinguishing the image presented at Sutton Hoo and that presented by Edward the Confessor was the full embrace of Roman Christianity (Figures 3 and 4). Membership of the Church offered kings a claim to Roman-ness, and universal authority. Kings increasingly emphasized their majesty while the structure of the Church became a way of placing loyal individuals throughout a territory. Churches and monasteries expressed a new form of royal power, in other words: that of Christian kings rather than warrior leaders.

Figure 4. Edward the Confessor (1042–1066)

The process took a long time, but there is little doubt about the imprint of Christianity on Anglo-Saxon kingship.

One way of tracing this more concretely is through the evolution of the Anglo Saxon law codes. They had a Germanic origin, and centred around personal restitution to victims—particularly, for example, payments to the family of victims of murder (wergild). These were carefully calibrated according to the status of the victim and reflected the high value placed on personal honour. Anglo-Saxon kings took a coronation oath which bound them to prevent robbery and rapine, but not vengeance killings, and their law codes similarly forbade robbery and rapine but not vengeance. On the other hand, they tried to limit the effects of vengeance, regulating it so as to prevent it making collective life unbearable.

For example, the law code of Alfred the Great (871–99) regulated vengeance by demanding that opponents, if possible, should be besieged for seven days and then allowed the possibility of surrender for a period of thirty days in which they could contact their kin and friends and make restitution. A hundred years later King Edmund's laws commanded that no one other than the slayer could be killed, and then only if wergild had not been paid.

Kings were thought to have a different role in relation to offences that affected the whole society rather than a single individual, however, and a recognized right to profit from any fines or compensation that were exacted. Robbery fell into this category because the victim could not be sure who the thief was, and because the suspicion and anxiety that theft creates affected the whole society, not just the immediate victims. So, too, did murder which, as a secret crime, harmed the king's peace. Homicide, where the perpetrator was known, remained a matter of personal honour, compensation, and restitution.

Christianity had an immediate and direct impact on these law codes: for example, Wihtred's code (695) not only included the clergy in the economy of compensation, but imposed penalties for those who had an adverse effect on society through failing to follow Christian values. Practising pagan sacrifice was now punishable and the code enforced the Christian form of marriage, sabbath observance, and banned meat eating during Lent. Kings were increasingly likely to present themselves as having a particular responsibility for the health of the Christian community and Christianity began to inflect other collective aspects of Anglo-Saxon law. The protection of the whole community, while present in Germanic codes, was gradually transformed into a sense that some wrongdoing represented an offence against God, the king, and the Christian community.[7] And it was not just kings that saw it this way: administration of the law was in the hands of local assemblies of free men that interpreted the codes and implemented them in the light of local conditions and expectations. It seems clear that among those expectations was a belief in Christian values of penance and submission.[8]

Christianity in fact had a deep effect on almost all aspects of Anglo-Saxon society, from changes in place-names and ideas of local belonging to what the Anglo-Saxons built and how they viewed their landscape. The new churches (minsters) and monasteries became focal points of spiritual life, and the many saint cults shaped feelings of local belonging and solidarity. But the Church also redrew local landscapes and networks, creating new associations and new focal points for social life. Minsters became central places—hubs of trade and manufacturing, as well as administration. Local churches evolved to create parochial identities, closely tied to local lordship, and later the manor and the township.

An idea that explains all dimensions of social life has the potential to actually affect all dimensions of social life and can create opportunities as well as exclusions. The Anglo-Saxon conversion, for example, probably created new opportunities for aristocratic women: the Oxford Dictionary of National Biography contains entries for about thirty-five women who were born or lived on Britain or Ireland between around 500 and 900. The largest portion of them are abbesses, nuns, and saints, who together outnumber the royal women listed. This is a tiny number, of course, but there are no other roles through which Anglo-Saxon women secure their place in that particular history book.[9]

Christian ideas exercised a fundamental influence on British life for centuries, of course. The Protestant reformation of the sixteenth century promoted new ideas about what a good Christian life consisted of, and therefore affected the life of households, as did religious revivals in the eighteenth and nineteenth centuries. This was true both for good and ill: Christian ideas have justified persecution of errant Christians, and other religious groups and also the subjection of non-Christian peoples, and played a role in the enslavement of Africans by British traders during the seventeenth and eighteenth centuries. On the other hand, Evangelical Christianity was a central strand of the campaign to end the slave trade, arguably the first mass movement in British history, and the effect was liberating for millions of people.

Such mobilizing ideas then can migrate well beyond the sphere in which they were first articulated, shaping family, neighbourhood, and workplace relations. Ideas of national greatness, egalitarianism, and economic efficiency can, for example, shape how children are brought up, how spouses and neighbours regard one another, and how co-workers are managed and appraised. Taken up, used, and interpreted by anyone exposed to them, they can have a life of their own which is outside the control of any individual or group, even if ideas are often most effective when supporting the interests of the powerful.

The Rise of Political Arithmetic and Political Economy

It is hard to explain much of modern political life without appreciating the importance of statistical thinking, but this is a habit of relatively recent origin. It was only around the turn of the eighteenth century that influential thinkers began to use numerical calculation systematically when thinking about social improvement. Through 'political arithmetic' they believed that the economy as a whole could be managed and that social improvement could be achieved through consciously promoted economic growth.[10]

Such a phenomenon is obviously complicated to understand, but it was not a product of material change, or of political ambition: it illustrates again the independent force of ideas on the uses of power. Statistical thinking took off in a number of areas of intellectual life and 'probabalistic' thinking underpinned a number of innovations such as insurance, for example. Rather than seek an absolute truth or certainty, people began to act on the basis of calculated risk, and the application of these ways of thinking to government, and the public good, had really profound implications. It was often applied in very prosaic ways: more precise mapping and counting shaped the way eighteenth-century governments managed public spaces, the streets, and beer production.[11] More ambitiously, public budgets began to weigh up costs and returns, allowing a quantified view of political issues from foreign policy to poor relief. In the nineteenth century the census and the Ordnance Survey extended these ambitions with a new comprehensiveness, underpinning a science of government: the belief that governments could understand, measure, and purposefully alter social life.

An element of that was sociological—that society could be understood in terms of the contribution of selected groups to the common good, or to social problems. In the last quarter of the nineteenth century, for example, this science of government was brought to bear on what was seen as the degeneration of the imperial 'race'. While Britannia dominated the globe and ruled the waves, there was increasing awareness of the feebleness of the

British population. Starting with Henry Mayhew's journalism in the 1840s, middle-class observers became increasingly concerned about the lives of the poor and by the time of Charles Booth and Seebohm Rowntree these concerns led to systematic enquiries into the condition of society.

Fear of degeneration was heightened by the scandal of recruitment for the South African War (1899–1902), when army medical officers judged three out of five volunteers unfit to serve. An Inter-Departmental Committee on Physical Deterioration (1904) was established to deal with the issue, while an Aliens Act sought to protect workers from competition by restricting immigration. Inspired by Rowntree and others, a new view of poverty took hold, reflecting habits of statistical thought, that while individuals bore some responsibility for their situation, other factors creating poverty were simply beyond their control. In a way, economists were discovering the idea of 'unemployment', along with the thought that government could alleviate it. Lloyd George's People's Budget of 1909 used government tax and spending power to begin to address these structural problems.

This is a world we recognize—of the coherent management of economic and social conditions by governments using their fiscal powers and informed by detailed statistical knowledge. In fact, political options are now routinely assessed in term of their effects on a single economic metric, Gross Domestic Product (GDP), invented by Simon Kuznets. During the 1930s, in response to a commission from the US Congress, he developed the Gross National Product as a simple measure of economic output. It was a calculation of the total worldwide output generated by US residents and was later replaced by the GDP, which measured the wealth generated within a nation's borders. It held an immediate appeal for politicians. For example, in 1960 John F. Kennedy stood for the US presidency on the promise of achieving annual growth of 5 per cent in GDP.[12] It is a very familiar style of politics—big decisions like Brexit, Scottish independence, and the election of a new government are all appraised against their potential effect on this single statistical measure. This is despite the fact that few voters know how it is produced, how these effects on its future values are modelled, or what effect GDP growth has on their own personal circumstances. Its rhetorical force reflects the power of a more fundamental idea— that a quantified science of government can deliver social progress.

There are many critiques of these statistical approaches, not least that what cannot be measured in these ways might still be a proper object of government. Nonetheless, the attraction of quantitative thinking has shaped political power just as dramatically as Christianity did in earlier centuries.

Conflict and Resistance

Ideas empower, but they also constrain. In thinking about their political effect, we don't have to decide whether or not they are true, or whether the people who espouse them are sincere (although those are both reasonable questions). What matters for the argument here is that they exert an influence on political life independent of dominant groups or individuals. For example, a monarch who appealed to Christian values in order to secure some new power may have been interested in the power, and to have been acting entirely cynically in appealing to Christian values to justify it. Having done so, however, he or she had to act in a way that was consistent with Christian values to appear credible. The power of ideas is independent of the intentions of the person who appeals to them: it depends in part on the audience for the appeal.[13] In fact, powerful ideas are not just reflected in political action; they can actually demand it. They have a life independent of dominant social groups, at least potentially, and for the same reason they can drive conflict and resistance.

Church and State: Religious and Political Obligations

A familiar example of this is changing ideas about the relationship between Church and state. Christianity played an important role in the consolidation of royal power in dynastic kingdoms from at least the eighth century onwards and shaped their politics for the following thousand years. But the source of Christian authority was not the monarchy—monarchs were believed to shelter the Church; it was not theirs. Moreover, monarchs could not simply define Christian ideas for their own purposes. The pressure created by Christian beliefs might lead them to pursue goals set by others and meet standards they would not have set for themselves.

There was also a further complication—these ideas originated in a separate, and potentially rival, set of institutions. The Church and its many component institutions generated their own income from the land and had an independent hold over the consciences and behaviour of the population. They had tenants and legal interests, resolved disputes, and enforced moral behaviour, offering a useful source of power to kings but also a potential rival.

During the eleventh century this potential conflict was brought into the open as a result of Pope Gregory VII's reforms, which tried to restore and extend the independent authority of the Papacy. One symptom of this was the investiture controversy, a stand-off over who should invest bishops; that is, confer their authority on them (no one doubted that kings should choose them). It was particularly acutely contested between the Papacy and the Holy Roman Emperor, in a series of conflicts that lasted forty years.

England had its own investiture controversy between 1102 and 1107, eventually resolved by the concordat of London, but the English Church and monarchy did not experience conflict on the same scale until Thomas Becket's Archbishopric, a century after the Gregorian reforms. Becket had been close to Henry II (1133–89)—he had served as chancellor and one of the king's sons had lived in his household—but once elected as archbishop in 1162 he defended the independent powers of the Church against royal pretensions, to Henry's fury. The issue that provoked the split was the right of members of the Church who had committed crimes ('criminous clerks') to be tried by Church courts rather than royal courts. By turns resistant, then compliant, then resistant, Becket infuriated the king, who had him convicted on trumped-up charges, and sentenced to forfeiture of his estates. Becket fled into exile for six years but returned in 1169 when the heir to the throne, Prince Henry, was crowned as heir apparent. Becket was determined to punish those clerics who had taken part in the ritual. His enemies told Henry II about his conduct, leading to the fateful words 'who will rid me of this turbulent priest?' and Becket's murder in Canterbury Cathedral by men eager to impress the king. Modern historians have been less impressed by Becket's claims to sainthood than were his contemporaries, but the conflict clearly arose out of jurisdictional frictions that were common across Europe (Figure 5).

Figure 5. The consecration of Thomas Becket, 1162

Over the following 500 years a succession of churchmen happily served the monarchy, evidently feeling no great difficulty in working for these two masters. The sixteenth-century reformation, however, created new tensions. Cardinal Wolsey, a highly effective royal servant as Chancellor, fell from grace in 1529 when he failed to secure the annulment of Henry VIII's marriage to Catherine of Aragon. This essentially political problem coincided with another movement for reform in the Church, this time directed primarily against the Papacy and its alleged corruption. The task of cleansing the Church of superstitious beliefs and practices was closely associated with an attack on clerical power, which was blamed for these corruptions. In the ensuing debates about what powers the clergy should have over believers, and what should be said and done in churches, attempts were also made to change the relationship between churches and states. Political convulsion ensued across Europe, and in England a series of churchmen lost their lives as one settlement of these issues followed another.

English monarchs emerged as heads of a national Church, and all administrative and financial ties between the English and Roman churches were cut. This royal supremacy was a two-edged sword, though, since subjects who disagreed with their monarch's religion might find their political obedience compromised as a result. There followed more than a century of trouble: a period we might refer to as that of 'reformation politics' in which there was a recurrent threat that disagreements over religious belief and practice might lead to political instability and that political divisions might arise from theological or doctrinal differences. The monarch had control of the institutions of the Church, but not what his or her subjects thought about the true religion. Dissenting groups challenged both the authority of the king in religion and the role of the national Church over their consciences.

The effects of reformation politics were not the same everywhere. In Scotland an aristocratic coup in the mid-sixteenth century aimed against French influence had also sided with the Protestant reformation. In sharp contrast to England, therefore, the Scottish reformation was not associated either with royal authority or the work of individual bishops. Instead it became associated with a Calvinist ideal of the Church, in which authority was built up from individual congregations and in some sense answered to them. Scottish subjects had pressed reform on their king and their bishops, and that more communal form of religion fitted that experience. But it was an uneasy settlement—there was a General Assembly which deliberated on the future of the Church, but had no independent legal powers, and so relied on the king and parliament and tensions persisted for three generations thereafter. They culminated in rebellion against a prayer book introduced by bishops at the prompting of the Crown, which by then was worn by a man permanently resident in England (see Chapter 5).

Ireland offers another contrast. The Norman kings of England had claimed authority in Ireland since the late twelfth century, when a concerted conquest had established a Lordship of Ireland. As Norman settlers assimilated to Irish society, though, the reality of this English authority had steadily diminished, and by the later middle ages it was largely confined to an area around Dublin known as the Pale. During the sixteenth century English monarchs had tried to strengthen their authority across the whole island by transforming the native aristocracy into courtly aristocrats like those familiar elsewhere in Europe, just as they were doing in England. By the middle of the century that effort had failed, and policy increasingly turned to colonization—planting a new society in Ireland and sweeping aside rebellious Irish lords. Protestantism in Ireland was actively promoted by the Elizabethan regime, but not in the Gaelic language, and it failed to take root—it was far less successful than movements for Catholic renewal. The failure of the reformation to take hold in Ireland drove a further wedge between Irish Lords and the English Crown, making the dynastic ambitions of the English Crown harder to achieve and leading to more concerted colonization.

These and many other convulsions in the history of Christianity reveal the potential of ideas to drive conflict and to limit the power of monarchs and others. They also show how the geography of those conflicts is not the same as that of the collective institutions on which they act, which further weakens the hold of any particular institution.

Diverse and Contested Ideas

Ideas have an independent influence both on the uses and the structure of collective institutions, but even the most dominant ideas do not generally achieve a monopoly. In fact, one source of dynamism in politics is the fact there is always a mix of ideas in play, to which people can appeal.

This influence can point powerfully in apparently bizarre directions. Following the execution of King Charles in 1649, the new regime, the commonwealth, not only abolished the House of Lords and the Church of England, but also passed acts against blasphemy and adultery, as well as a Navigation Act, requiring colonies exporting particular goods to do so using English ships. To what problem is the following the answer: the death penalty for adultery and blasphemy, and the compulsory use of English shipping for the export of 'goods or commodities of the growth, production or manufacture of Asia, Africa or America' to England?[14] It is not plain why a new government would have these priorities, and hard to explain without reference to dominant ideas. Both these priorities—moral reformation and economic regulation—can be interpreted as exercises in control, and as the expression of the interest of powerful groups, but they were justified in different ways and offered different reasons for political action: one to demonstrate the godly credentials of the regime and to assuage God's anger with the nation; the other to project English power against other European states. Even in this crisis situation the new regime was responding to more than one mobilizing idea.[15]

More obvious tensions between dominant ideas can limit the power of any particular idea. Aristocratic honour and loyalty to the monarch, for example, created tensions for elite individuals throughout the period of the dynastic kingdoms. Whatever his personal ambitions (and failings), it is clear that Christian faith and personal honour were important to Simon De Montfort, one of the best known of England's baronial challengers to royal authority, whose efforts to restrain Henry III (1216–72) were of long-lasting significance. Henry had alienated many of his most important subjects through his choice of advisers, and this came to matter when his unpopular decisions seemed to confirm the consequences of having the wrong advice. In 1254 he accepted the offer of Sicily from the Pope to provide for his second son, on condition that he would pay for its conquest and pay off the Pope's debts. The expense of this deal (which probably was not a very good one) prompted leading barons to take power from his hands in 1258. In cooperation with parliament formal limits were placed on his powers by the Provisions of Oxford (1258) and of Westminster (1259). This in turn prompted civil war over whether the king should be free to choose his own advisers.

De Montfort was the champion of the reform programme. He had proven his Christian credentials as a crusader and by expelling Jews from Leicester. In power he cancelled Henry's debts and saw Jewish creditors murdered. He was undoubtedly motivated by all sorts of things, but a strong (if repellent) Christian faith was clearly one of them. This commitment to the public good and Christian reform led him to a nasty end at the 'battle' of Evesham, where a band of men were roaming the field with the express intention of killing him. De Montfort's personal honour led him to a gory death: hearing that his son had been killed, he reportedly said, 'then it is time to die', before leading a doomed charge ending in his death and dismemberment. This was closely connected with his religious views, though. Shortly before his head was cut off, and slightly longer before his severed testicles were placed either side of his nose, he is reported to have said, 'Thank God'. His personal honour and vision of good government mattered more to him than loyalty to the monarch or his own life. This is a dramatic demonstration of tensions that many important aristocrats felt throughout the period when political life was framed by dynastic kingdoms.

The complex interaction of mobilizing ideas matters because the failure of ideas to take hold, or to persuade people, can severely limit the effectiveness of collective institutions. What can be achieved at any one time is partly determined by the extent to which mobilizing ideas actually convince people, and there is a long history of the rejection of these dominant ideas, or the sincerity of those who promoted them. It seems, for example, that the commonwealth's Adultery Act was unenforceable (or at least barely enforced) for this reason—the death penalty that some educated men thought matched the gravity of the sin did not at all match popular views about the seriousness of the actual behaviour.[16] There is also a long history of 'social crime': the indulgence of forms of behaviour formally defined as criminal but which were more or less acceptable to most people, such as small-scale smuggling and tax evasion by paying for small jobs in cash. In the case of drug policy, this may have led to changes in policing, for example deciding that it was not worth prosecuting people for the possession of small amounts of cannabis.

Since at least the early twentieth century there has been a similar concern about voters' disengagement from national democratic politics and the existence of 'anti-politics'. The mobilizing claims about the public good made by politicians in the democratic age have always sounded hollow to some voters. In 1919, a year after the establishment of universal male suffrage and partial female suffrage, Arnold Freeman, a committed socialist and reformer, led a survey of the working classes in Sheffield to gauge their 'adequacy' for the 'discharge of their responsibilities as heads of households, producers and citizens'. The team interviewed more than 800 male and female workers and assessed their responses against five standards: well-equipped, semi-well-equipped, inadequately equipped, semi-mal-equipped, and mal-equipped. The last three categories were a comfortable majority, and a key theme in their responses was indifference or active suspicion and hostility to politics and politicians.[17]

A research project at the University of Southampton has traced these things since the 1930s and the conduct of Mass Observation exercises which sought to drop in on the conversations and opinions of ordinary men and women. Again, this strain of anti-politics is present, and is also revealed by opinion polling and sampling in the 1940s. Even in 1944, with the country at war, 35 per cent of respondents in one poll thought politicians were out 'merely for themselves' and another 22 per cent thought they were out for their party. In 1945 42 per cent of voters disapproved of politicians for their vote-catching stunts, mud-slinging, and the slight attention paid to policy (that is, what they would actually do if elected). Mass Observation evidence for 1945 suggested that conversations about politicians often portrayed them as self-seeking, place-seeking, 'gas-bags', and 'gift-of-the-gabbers'.[18] Many voters seem unconvinced by the promises of representative democracy, and those seeking power through it.

* * *

Those who control collective institutions do not control the ideas that legitimate them, or how people interpret them. Ideas can animate active opposition, rival claims to power and provide an active restraint on differential power. There are more examples of how ordinary people took advantage of this potential in Chapter 6, but it is a familiar phenomenon. From the fourteenth century onwards prosecutions and reports of seditious speech reveal at least the potential for subversive views of the claims of monarchs and great men, and for the development of an alternative view of how the world should work.[19]

But majorities can also be tyrannous. The force of Christian ideas, for example, had implications for the attitudes towards other religious groups. For example, as we have seen, Simon De Montfort's assertion of his Christian values was partly expressed in a repugnant and murderous hostility to the Jews. This kind of hostility led eventually to their expulsion in 1290, while their readmission to England in the 1650s was linked to the hope that conversion to Christianity would be a prelude to the return of Christ and the saints. A legacy of reformation politics, however, was a suspicion of those who did not share the national faith. In 1753 legislation was introduced to make it easier for Jews to be naturalized—it would have meant that they could take the oath of allegiance to the monarch, and the oath of supremacy recognizing the monarch's headship of the Church without having to swear 'on the true faith of a Christian'. It faced intense popular hostility, however, expressed in petitions and in a lurid press campaign—and it was repealed in 1754 for fear of its impact on the election due that year.[20] Divisions among Christians have been equally powerful. Catholics and some Protestants, as well as Jews, were formally excluded from public office until the repeal of the Test and Corporation Acts in 1828 and the Catholic Relief Act of the following year. Informal discrimination continued long after, of course, and still persists.

One of the criticisms of statistical approaches to the business of government is therefore that government by simple majorities does not lead to the representation of all interests in society. John Stuart Mill wrote about this, arguing that representation ought to hold a mirror to the whole of society, not just express the aggregate will of the majority.[21] This issue was in play, although not really stated this way, in the debate about how to interpret the result of the 2016 Brexit referendum. The majoritarian interpretation of the relatively narrow majority for Brexit (52:48) was that it gave a mandate to leave on any terms (or none); the counter-case that whole regions (interests) had not voted for Brexit (such as majorities in Scotland and Northern Ireland). Such is the power of numbers now that they are thought to speak for themselves in political matters, despite all the evidence to the contrary.

Finally, we have already noted the geographical aspect of this, the implications of which are developed in Chapter 5, that political change has often been driven by powerful ideas which originated beyond Great Britain: the arrival and transformation of Christian values, the impact of the investiture controversy, or the reformation, for example. The Catholic plotters who famously tried to blow up the English parliament in 1605 were motivated by the need to bring the country back to obedience to Rome and, since the 1790s, and the aftershocks of the French revolution, UK governments have periodically been worried by the influence of (foreign) revolutionary ideas on political life.

Ideas are central to the history of politics. They prompt action—for example, leading to the imposition of the death penalty for adultery as an expression of a new republic's responsibility to combat sin. They make powerful people do things they do not want to do. They define a problem in a particular way—leading people to talk about the virtues of the EU, for example, in terms of GDP. And they offer resources to call the powerful to account but also license forms of social exclusion. Their geography does not map neatly on the geography of the institutions they help to animate. If ideas shape how collective institutions are used and regulated, it follows that changing the patterns of political life probably requires changing attitudes and beliefs.

3

MATERIAL CONDITIONS AND THE USES OF COLLECTIVE INSTITUTIONS

'Real' factors such as economic complexity, climate change, and disease are equally important in shaping the use of collective institutions, and new technologies can enable or demand new kinds of political action: for example, the advent of writing or the possibilities of Big Data. This chapter looks at the varying role of such material factors in shaping the uses of political power. It sets out some examples of how economic change drove political change: the transition from hunter-gathering to farming; the changing geography of trade and exchange; and the growth of global interdependence in the aftermath of industrialization. But it also shows how political arrangements can make some forms of economic activity possible or impossible, a point illustrated through the history of the slave trade: the relationship between economic complexity and collective institutions is reciprocal, not simply one-way. It also explores the impact of environmental change and the relationship between collective institutions and technological change. As with economic complexity, this latter relationship works in both directions: collective institutions do not simply take advantage of technological change; they can also help foster it.

Economic Change and Political Complexity

Hunter-Gatherers, Farmers, and Traders

Until about 10,000 years ago, the human presence in this part of Europe was made up of bands of hunter-gatherers. We know from observation that such groups exercise collective power which depends on cooperation—they achieve as groups what they could not achieve as individuals. Collective action is central to the hunting of big game, for example, and the cave art that hunter-gatherers across Europe have left, including at Cresswell Crags, on the Nottinghamshire/Derbyshire border, suggests that this was an important aspect of their collective lives. In general, though, hunter-gatherers leave hardly any permanent mark on the landscape. For the bulk of the time that humans have been on Britain, therefore, we can say very little about their collective life: the art at Cresswell is at least 13,000 years old, but probably dates from a very late phase of hunter-gathering.[1]

As we saw in in the Introduction, the end of hunter-gathering might in that sense be the most dramatic change in collective life in British history. Climatic improvement was followed by the adoption of farming, something associated around the globe with the development of the 'early state'. Agrarian societies are assumed to be more heavily governed than hunter-gatherer societies, and in fact one mystery being addressed in current scholarship is why humans opted for agriculture, which is more work than hunting and gathering, possibly less healthy, and also has this cost in accepting the authority of government and a loss of personal agency.[2] However we eventually come to explain that, the effects of that change in the archaeological record are dramatic: the end of hunting and gathering is closely and quickly associated on Britain with a dramatic change in the evidence of collective action. Recent scholarship has again suggested that this relationship is more complicated than once thought. Not only was there was a long lag between the adoption of farming and the development of state-like organizations, there are also sites where a ritual centre attracted settlement and large-scale collective projects among people who had not adopted farming: it may even be that in some places it was the accumulation of population at a ritual site led to the adoption of farming, rather than vice versa.[3] Nonetheless, although there may not be an exclusive relationship between concentrations of population, large-scale collective building, and farming, there does seem to be a powerful connection.

Trade has also exercised a profound influence on collective institutions. Long-distance trade in precious commodities was well established by the end of the Neolithic period and increased in the Bronze Age, leading elites on Britain to engage with the Roman empire and even to help support their military effort. That part of Great Britain that was eventually under direct Roman rule was directly integrated into a much wider world of production and exchange, producing a sharp contrast in the archaeological record with that part of the island beyond Roman rule. This economic transformation is discussed in more detail in the next chapter, but it illustrates how trade affects not just the structure, but also the geography of power.

This relationship is clear in the history of the post-Roman period. During the ninth century the arrival of Viking raiders on the east coast of England, north coast of Scotland, and both coasts of the Irish sea was part of a broader expansion, which took them to the west coast of Iceland. By the end of the century they were on the shores of the Caspian Sea. Baghdad, Iran, Afghanistan, and central Asia were connected to this expanding diaspora, something reflected in the presence of silver Islamic coins (Dirhams) in archaeological sites in Scandinavia and on Britain. During the tenth century they reached the west coast of Greenland and beyond, northern France, and were established along a corridor from the Baltic to the Black Sea. By then Viking settlers farming the land and driving the trade in towns in northern and western Britain connected the island to a very extensive trade network, reaching from Kiev to the shores of north America. The archaeology reveals these wide trading connections: walrus ivory, steatite, soapstone, amber, schist, and wine were imported from Scandinavia and across Europe, and silk from further afield.

The defeat of the Vikings did not sever the connections between Britain and Europe. The Kingdom of England was connected to north-east Europe by dynastic interests and over the following centuries trade connections further south were of central importance to England's politics: cloth, wine, and salt, along with metals, ceramics, and leather; and, later, silk, sugar, rice, almonds, and oriental spices. Ambition and the pursuit of wealth drew Britons to Flanders, the Rhine, Aquitaine, and a little later the Mediterranean. For 500 years the English Crown had extensive commercial and political interests in France. But, on the other hand, the political interests of the Kingdoms of England and Scotland continually extended beyond their borders—the geography of political ambition followed trade and other economic opportunities, pursued through conquest and shrewd marriage.

There was a major shift in this geography when long-distance oceanic trade between Europe and the Americas opened up during the sixteenth century, although the English kingdom was not a major player in this expansion until the middle of the seventeenth century, and the Scottish kingdom later than that. The crisis of the English civil war, as we have seen, created taxing and spending power on a scale that could shape economic activity. This power was almost immediately put to the service of empire, for example through the creation of the Navigation system tying the trade of the colonies in particular commodities to the home market under the protection of English naval power. Backed by this fiscal and military apparatus, English (and later UK) economic and naval power extended around the entire globe over the following three centuries.

This was not just a factor shaping the geography of political ambition, but something that shaped opportunities for individuals. The nexus of overseas trade and government contracting, for example, created new ways to get rich in the seventeenth century. Sir Martin Noell rose from apparent obscurity to become a major merchant and government creditor during the 1640s and 1650s. He was a government contractor for the army and navy, supplying beds, blankets, and saltpetre (essential for making gunpowder). During the 1650s he 'farmed' the excise taxes—paying the government a sum up front and recouping his investment (and turning a profit) by collecting the tax himself—and he later made a similar arrangement for the Post Office. He also invested his accelerating profits in Barbados, helping to provide the capital which transformed it into the first British slave society and through his family establishing extensive trade and agricultural interests. Sir Stephen Fox came to a similar arrangement a decade later, agreeing to raise the money to pay the army while the government waited for tax revenues to come in. He took a commission of 5 per cent and was also compensated for the interest he had to pay to borrow the money. As he ploughed his commission back into the scheme, though, he needed to borrow less, so that the allowance for interest became a kind of super-profit, and as he increasingly used his own money rather than borrowing to pay the soldiers, his profits expanded continually. He too was able to buy farms of revenues, so that he was taking a personal profit both on government income and expenditure. From rather humble origins and a position of penury in the 1650s, he became the richest commoner in England by the 1680s, far richer than many aristocrats.[4]

People who never scaled such heights found more modest benefits in the system. Just as the Roman empire offered an opportunity as well as a threat for those at its edges, the Scottish parliament voted for Union partly in order to get full access to the nascent British empire. As a consequence of the expansion of overseas trade and settlement, more and more Britons led global lives, while from the sixteenth century domestic consumption normalized the use of many exotic products—potatoes, tea, coffee, sugar, chocolate, and cotton, for example.[5]

The Slave Trade: How Collective Power Shapes Economic Exchange

Some of the biggest changes in patterns of collective life have therefore been determined by changes in economic behaviour—the switch from hunter-gathering to farming, for example, or broad changes in the geography of power which reflect shifting patterns of trade. The slave trade, however, illustrates particularly graphically how the opposite is also true: that collective institutions profoundly shape patterns of economic behaviour.

The first English slave trader, John Hawkins, operated as an individual, trading enslaved Africans during the 1560s. For a long period thereafter the English merchants who engaged in African trade were interested in natural commodities—the gold and ivory, for example, which have given English names to parts of the African coast. It was in the mid-seventeenth century that the slave trade really took off, a way to deal with a labour shortage in the booming sugar industry on Barbados, establishing a system of production that was then extended to other newly founded colonies.

This connection with colonization reflects the role of the government in fostering the slave trade. From 1660 onwards merchants trading with Africa were given a monopoly on the supply of slaves, a way of safeguarding their profits, and in 1698 the British trade was opened up to all British merchants. This helped cement the UK's place as the leading state in the slave trade, alongside Portugal, through the eighteenth century. Ultimately British merchants shipped more than 3 million people from Africa to slave markets in the Caribbean and North America, and elsewhere. Of them only around 2.7 million survived the dreadful conditions on board the slave ships. Active government intervention had fostered and protected this appalling trade, and first London, then Bristol and Liverpool, boomed on its profits (Figure 6).

All this human misery depended on being able to treat enslaved people as commodities, and that was a political, moral, and legal decision: it is clearly not a neutral fact of economic life. This is a more general point: a 'free market' is not something naturally occurring, but a legal and political construct. There is much more to it than the existence of supply and demand. It requires enforceable contracts, usually negotiated on the basis of agreement about standards, weights and measures, and so on. If a market is to

Figure 6. Enslaved Africans cutting cane in Antigua, 1823

operate smoothly, consumers need to know in advance what they are buying, for how much, and that they can have redress if they are mis-sold or sold short. This contrasts sharply with production, distribution, and consumption outside a free market. There redress may not be available, or only available through force—the thought that supplies the central dramatic tension in depictions of the drug market in numerous books, films, or TV series.

The really key point is that we only construct free markets in things we are happy to see traded as commodities. The slave trade is surely the most shocking example of this in British history— the view that a human can be traded as a commodity—but it also illustrates how these political and ethical judgements vary over time. As we have seen, the end of the slave trade owed a lot to the force of Evangelical Christianity—a moral repugnance leading to

abolition. There are many other examples of how collective institutions can facilitate or suppress economic activity. For example,
it was for a long time thought immoral to trade money in this way,
and attitudes towards the circulation of pornographic images
have changed dramatically in recent years. In other words, behind
a free market lie value judgements. Should I be able to sell my kid-
ney, for which there is both supply and demand? Is education a
commodity which should be traded in a free market? Such questions are not new.

In this context it is helpful to think about forms of economic
behaviour rather than 'the economy'. The economy is a term for
the aggregate effect of individual actions and choices, but collective institutions can allow or prevent aggregate effects of individual action by shifting patterns of behaviour in the interests of
the general good. This is not just a matter of allowing or disallow-
ing the trade in humans, body parts, or pornographic images. It
also allows collective action to address problems arising from
behaviour which carries no obvious immediate disadvantage for
individuals but which is harmful at an aggregate level—throwing
waste into a river, driving a heavily polluting car, selling unafford-
able mortgages, or over-fishing. Collective institutions can also
address what is often referred to as the free-rider problem—the need
to achieve something beneficial for everyone, and all businesses for
example, which no one or no business has sufficient incentive to
undertake. We will all take a free ride if we can, and again institutions can solve that problem for the general good. In other words,
economic behaviour and new possibilities interact with political
arrangements and beliefs, rather than simply determining them,
or being determined by them. Economic and political complexity

continually intertwine: collective institutions are not simply driven by economic 'reality'; they help create it.

Industrialization and Global Interdependence

Shifting patterns of trade helped shape the overall geography and ambition of political systems, as well as the opportunities for people living within them (for better and for much, much worse). But the geography of collective institutions has never mapped neatly onto the geography of economic connection.

This has been even more obviously true in more recent times. During the nineteenth century rapid industrialization and globalizing markets created new collective problems. At root, these developments meant that the fate of people living on Great Britain became increasingly closely connected with developments taking place well beyond the reach of UK governments. Industrialization, driven first by cotton and then by heavy industry, depended on long-distance trade—for example, the import of raw cotton and then the export of the cloth to profitable markets around the world. During the 1870s the 2 per cent of the world's population that lived on Britain produced 40 per cent of the world's manufactured goods, while British investment underlay industrialization all around the world. British engineers and capital drove railway-building on three continents, for example.

At home there was massive population growth and urbanization, as an army of wage labour clustered around new and ever-larger factories. In 1851 the population of Britain and Ireland had reached 27.4 million, and it increased to 41.5 million over the next fifty years. Textiles were the third largest employer in the UK in 1881, behind agriculture and domestic service, and metal industries were not far behind. This huge and rapidly growing urban population also became dependent on imported food. Whereas in 1868 the UK produced 80 per cent of its own food, only thirty years later it imported 75 per cent of its cereals and 40 per cent of its meat. This was partly a product of the influx of cheap food imports from the rapidly growing US agricultural sector, itself fuelled by cheap transport that was a product of the industrial revolution.

By the third quarter of the nineteenth century British industry traded from a position of enormous strength and was at the heart of a global trading system held together by British capital, ships, and telegraph cables. For the same reason, though, the UK economy had become more exposed to shocks arising from parts of the globe over which the UK had no direct control. One example of this is the Cotton Famine of the 1860s. By that time around 80 per cent of the UK's cotton imports were produced by enslaved people on the Southern US plantations. Finished cotton accounted for about 35 per cent of UK exports, and whole towns, and even regions, depended on the health of the industry. The consequences of this interdependence became clear as a result of the American civil war in the 1860s. The Southern Confederates initially imposed an export ban in order to pressure the UK government to support their cause. This was succeeded by a northern blockade of the South intended to choke its economy, which also cut off supplies to the UK. As a result, the price of raw cotton soared, and British workers were laid off or put on short time in huge numbers. By the end of 1862 half a million cotton workers were on poor relief and in the following year, in Stalybridge (then in Cheshire), for example, 7,000 of the town's 25,000 workers were out of work: collateral damage of the American civil war.

However, if global interdependence created this problem, it also offered a solution. High prices for raw cotton encouraged British investment in production elsewhere, notably Egypt and India. Output in Egypt rose five-fold between 1850 and 1880 and in India exports to the UK tripled between 1860 and 1866. This quickly replaced dependence on US exports with dependence on India, a relationship captured by the famous image of Gandhi visiting the Lancashire cotton towns during the 1930s. As he put it, Indian peasants and Lancashire factory hands earned pennies making cloth for rich Indians, and his campaign for Indian independence placed great symbolic weight on a campaign for Indians to use homespun cloth (Figure 7).

The mobility of capital and the pressure to find good further returns on the profits being generated by industry was another

Figure 7. Mohandas Gandhi with textile workers in Darwen, Lancashire, 1931

source of vulnerability, however. In 1873 over-investment in rail stock led to a financial crash in the Viennese stock market which quickly spread to other markets. European investors, enticed by the massive programme of railway building in the US, had driven the price of rail stock to a level at which confidence collapsed cata-strophically. Stock and rail bond prices now fell drastically all over the world, bringing bank failures and depression in their wake. In the UK the Bank of England raised its bank rate to 9 per cent to protect its reserves—7 per cent higher than in previous decades.

While the UK was protected from some of the most dramatic consequences of the crisis, it nonetheless helped redirect British investments, particularly towards Africa, Latin America, and the white settler colonies. However, there was now competition. The unification of Germany and its rapid industrialization created competition for global markets, as did the rapid growth of the US economy. By 1916 US GDP equalled that of the entire British empire, reflecting the returns produced by the internal colonization of North America in the 'opening of the West' (for white settlers). The emergence of Italy and Japan as unified and industrializing powers also had implications, not just for the UK but for France and Russia too. While US investment could be productive in the colonization of the West, European powers looked for investment returns outside their borders, notably in Africa. Between 1870 and 1914 the proportion of the continent formally colonized by European powers rose from around 10 per cent to 90 per cent.

Globalizing markets and the mobility of capital were not the only sources of increased interdependence. A critical element of industrialization was the shift from dependence on muscle power and organic raw materials to mineral energy and metals: from organic to mineral-based energy. It was this 'carbon revolution' that made the transformation of productivity possible. It is now seen as one of the main ways in which human activity is having a major impact on the planet, contributing to global warming. Some scholars and commentators in fact refer to this as a distinctive geological era—the Anthropocene, in which planetary conditions are significantly affected by the activity of a single species—and its origins are traced directly to Britain.[6] Energy-intensive activity in one place creates environmental impacts well beyond the borders of the state in which it sits. This too has added to the growing importance of global interdependencies and created pressure for international cooperation and arbitration.

The importance of electricity to these transformations is not so often recognized. Firstly, and critically, it made energy portable, so that it could be stored and consumed far from the point at which it was generated. This was important to many twentieth-century technologies—no animal power was necessary to drive a record player or fax machine; indeed there was no need for a nearby energy generation at all. Secondly, it was increasingly used to carry information more or less instantaneously over large, effectively global, distances. This has allowed the phenomenal mobility of capital in creating another source of global interdependence. The portability of power and information are both features of the modern world which separate it from generations of earlier technological change, and they have forged close connections between the fate of populations separated by national borders.

Inter-State Cooperation: From Westphalia to the EU

Global economic interdependence has been a key motor of increased political action at larger scales—that is, of inter-state cooperation. This was not in itself new to industrial Europe, however, and is often traced back to the era of the reformation. The legacy of Rome and the successor kingdoms in central Europe was a loosely connected Holy Roman Empire, made up of a myriad of local principalities and free states. The sixteenth-century reformation had different outcomes in each of them so that these German-speaking lands resembled a patchwork of religious and political identities. Among them were a smaller number of states that had the right to elect the Emperor, and control of these electorates was important for dynastic and religious ambition. During the 1610s a disputed succession in Bohemia, because of its effects on the balance of electoral politics, became critical to the fate of the empire and European Protestantism. Foreign powers weighed in on the dispute, and the empire became the focus of what became the Thirty Years' War. It was marked by its intensity—measured, for example, by the scale of deaths on battlefields—but also by the price paid by the civilian population. The cost of the presence of these armies was enormous and they were willing to inflict appalling suffering on populations that were foreign to them, or distinct in their religion.

The various powers in the empire itself and the foreign powers that had intervened could not achieve peace by a series of bi-lateral agreements. The result was the Peace of Westphalia, signed in 1648, seen by political scientists as the origins of a system for securing international diplomatic and security order through multilateral agreements: the Westphalian system. That system has been used for more and more purposes since it emerged as a solution to the peculiar horrors of the Thirty Years' War: for example, at the Congress of Vienna at the end of the Napoleonic Wars.

The European colonization of Africa, for example, was governed by principles agreed among the major European powers at the Berlin Conference in 1884 and 1885—possession, more or less, was agreed to constitute sovereignty. This brought order not just to international diplomacy through inter-governmental cooperation—as had been done at the peace of Westphalia or Vienna—but also to the global economy.

During the twentieth century, the increasingly obvious connection between diplomatic and economic order led to an expansion of this sphere of inter-governmental cooperation. After the crisis of the First World War a multi-lateral settlement was signed at Versailles. It included agreement to establish the League of Nations to promote cooperation and arbitration in order to safeguard the peace: a permanent inter-governmental body responsible for sustaining the international order. The great crash of 1929 reverberated around an ever more integrated global economy, and the League of Nations began to see global economic stability as of equal importance to open diplomacy and the world peace.[7] Following the Second World War inter-state organizations took an even more active role in global economic management, including the support of liberal market economies—the UN and its agencies, the Marshall plan, the European Coal and Steel Community, and the General Agreement on Tariffs and Trade (GATT) all aimed at securing prosperity through economic cooperation at an international level. The creation of the World Bank was similarly a tool both for global economic management and domestic 'reform'.

Inter-state cooperation has had sharp limits where the perceived interests of national governments are concerned, however. No government is eager to sign up to international agreements that will make their populations poorer, and the effects on GDP of environmental regulation, for example, have led to considerable problems in getting inter-governmental cooperation on the issue. As a result, the differential power of these inter-state organizations is tightly limited by the participating governments. Fundamentally these inter-state organizations were created to promote growth, stability, and security in an increasingly interdependent world, and their actions reflect the aggregate effect of inter-state agreement around the table. Frustration with that has led to mobilization outside these institutions to influence decisions within them, and attempts to create a public which can hold these larger organizations to account in the way that each of the constituent governments are.

These economic changes increasingly affected the whole globe, and those wider global entanglements are essential to understanding collective life on Great Britain. One minor example of this is the place of the proceeds of slave ownership in philanthropic and infrastructure projects in the UK during the nineteenth century. The Conwy suspension bridge in North Wales, for example, was partly financed by John Gladstone (1784–1851). He had begun life trading to Calcutta but then made a sizeable fortune in Virginia tobacco and grain. As his wealth increased, he diversified further, including into sugar production in the slave colony of Guiana. He also argued publicly with the abolitionist James Cropper. There are many such examples: not least Edward Colston, Bristol slave trader and philanthropist, whose memorialization was at the centre of controversy in the Black Lives Matter campaign of 2020. In fact, Sir Joseph Bazalgette, mastermind of the London sewers, came from a family that had made money from investments in the slave trade, as did Sir James Hogg, chairman of the Metropolitan Board of Works in the later nineteenth century.[8]

Empire connected the fates of populations across the globe, and shaped the development of British society, but (it hardly needs to be said) the relationships were highly unequal. In managing the European colonization of Africa, the Berlin Conference was regulating a global development—the mobility of European capital in an increasingly globalized economy—while taking account only of European voices.

Environmental Change and Collective Institutions

Economic production and exchange are not the only material factors that shape political life, of course. There is a growing awareness of the effects of environmental conditions on human societies from the earliest periods of human settlement. The rhythm of the hunter-gatherer presence in this area of Europe was driven by the climate, as groups were drawn north by the herds which they preyed in periods when the ice had retreated. Putting the evidence of human tools or remains together with evidence about climate change and of the flora and fauna of Britain suggests that the human presence was intermittent, responsive to changing environmental conditions. The earliest evidence of human presence dates from a relatively warm period 900,000–500,000 years ago when the ice retreated and animals moved north into what was then an extension of the north European land mass. Stone tools found at Happisburgh, on the Norfolk coast, might be over 900,000 years old, the oldest stone tools found north of the Alps. Those found a little further south at Pakefield, on the Suffolk coast, are more recent, but still very ancient. These early humans probably followed the Rhine north to a large open bay, crossing

87

to southern Britain via a chalk ridge, then following the lost river Bytham upstream. There they were in the company of hippos and other now exotic species. Human remains about 500,000 years old have been found at Boxgrove, West Sussex, but from about 470,000 years ago ice returned as far south as the Thames, an extent that persisted for 60,000 years. A relatively brief inter-glacial followed and a human presence can be detected again, notably at Swanscombe, Kent. The ice then returned again until around 230,000 years ago and when it retreated there is evidence of Neanderthal presence. Ice returned once more about 180,000 years ago and humans seem to have been entirely absent for about 100,000 years. Neanderthals returned about 70,000 years ago but had lost out to modern humans by about 40,000 years ago. From 10,000 years ago modern humans dominate the archaeological record, and there was a dramatic improvement in climate from around then.

Climate change may have had a dramatic impact on human activity at other periods too. It has been linked with a wide var-iety of social and political phenomena during the Little Ice Age (dated roughly from around 1300 to around 1800), for example, including global political instability during the seventeenth cen-tury. That 'General Crisis' embraced changes of political regime between 1640 and 1660 in England, France, Catalonia, Portugal, Naples, Turkey, China, and India. Across the century as a whole, we could add Russia and Japan to the list. A fall of 2°C in global average temperatures is credited with causing colder winters and wetter summers in northern Europe. That in turn led to falling agricultural output and made governing more difficult. These environmental conditions are not generally accepted as primary causes of political crisis but are broadly accepted to have been a factor which cannot be ignored.[9]

The impact of environmental change is often easier to see at smaller scales, however. At Flag Fen, near Peterborough, a causeway 1km long was built about 3,500 years ago using 60,000 timbers, and maintained and upgraded several times over 400 years. Although it seems to have had a ritual and not simply functional significance, it was at least partly a collective response to rising water levels.[10] Nearby there is a section of Roman road, the Fen Causeway, and excavations there suggest that later phases of construction were also responses to environmental change, attempts to overcome periodic inundation.

In later periods we can see more clearly the political effects of changing environmental conditions. At Dunwich, on the Suffolk coast, the movement of the estuary led to the abandonment of the harbour. There followed legal disputes between the corporation of Dunwich and the neighbouring lords of Walberswick which involved not just attempts to settle various issues about rights and duties, but also thinking about how to measure and mark the landscape and administrative boundaries.[11] During the Little Ice Age there is evidence of the effects of increased storminess on agricultural output in the highlands and Western Isles. Farming on higher ground was abandoned, as tenants were unable to make enough (on average) to subsist and also reliably meet rent payments. Elsewhere the chief threat was not falling temperature, but runs of bad harvests caused by storminess, and this could be offset by temporary easing of rent demands.[12] Clearly, local arrangements can be responsive to environmental change and, to some extent, limit its effects.

Environmental change can be the result of human activity, of course, and human behaviour can pose serious environmental challenges as, for example, with the problem of human waste in London from the sixteenth to the nineteenth centuries. England had a very early experience of environmental degradation associated with industrial activity and the carbon revolution. In the early seventeenth century the village of Whickham in Northumberland was turned inside out. A generation previously it had been a reasonably prosperous agricultural community, living on a mix of arable and pastoral farming. The presence of coal close to the Tyne and shipping routes to London, however, created a significant commercial opportunity. A new lease of coal mining rights in the manor was granted in the late sixteenth century, the Grand Lease, which eventually came into the hands of major coal merchants in Newcastle. By the second decade of the seventeenth century they were making much more aggressive use of their rights to dig for coal and to transport it across the land. Wagon ways were built to get the coal to the river efficiently and after 1610 growing demand prompted very rapid, perhaps reckless, development, often in competition with owners of mines not covered by this Grand Lease. A survey in 1620 complained that over the previous decade 150 new pits had been dug not only in wastes and common land, but in arable fields too. Of those, more than 120 had already been abandoned, while new ones were being dug all the time. None were fenced in, and both men and animals were injured or killed by falls. The waste from the pits caused further loss of arable land, as did the construction of new coalways. Trenches and sluices undermined houses and drained the twenty wells that the manor had previously boasted. In all, more than a third of the township 'is laid quite waste and yields not, nor cannot yield any profit at all by reason of the said pits and rubbish lying about them'.[13]

At the other end of the process was London, which by 1600 had become dependent on coal. By then it was common for Londoners to complain of the smoke and attempts were made to limit its effects on the environment and human health by treating it in law as a nuisance and making polluters responsible for the damage they were causing. In 1624 Charles I had introduced legislation to try to control the smoke emission from numerous breweries in Westminster and the quality of London's air remained a concern for centuries thereafter, indeed up to the time of writing. In 1819 Michael Angelo Taylor, MP, introduced a bill to work out what might be done to mitigate the smoke he claimed 'clouded the atmosphere', causing 'prejudice to public health and private comfort'. Now, though, the problems in London were seen as a problem shared with the whole country. The famous smog of December 1952 contributed to the deaths of 20,000 people and prompted what became the Clean Air Act of 1956.[14] That was an undoubted success and an example of how collective institutions can contribute to the handling of environmental change, whether human-made or otherwise.

The congregation of humans has produced environmental problems throughout the recorded past—not least in public health—and the main sewer in Rome, the *Cloaca Maxima,* for example, was an enterprise envied by Victorian reformers. The self-organizing complexity arising from economic behaviour—making, buying, and selling—may not always be sustainable over the long term. This is related to the free-rider problem: that some actions are essential to sustainable living but none of us on our own has sufficient incentive to make them happen.

Both issues are exacerbated by the scale and range of human environmental impacts. This has continued to increase since the early industrial revolution in England and can have effects across much larger global regions: the nuisance caused by industrial activity now extends well beyond state borders. Britain's experience of the carbon revolution was to some extent formative for the Anthropocene: in fact, the term Anglocene has been coined to capture that contribution to the larger transformation. The UK and the USA were responsible for the lion's share of carbon emissions up to 1980.[15] As that term makes clear, though, this was nonetheless part of an increasingly shared global history. The effects of sulphur emissions in causing acid rain were first identified in Manchester in the 1850s and the effects of British emissions on the Norwegian environment had been identified as early as the 1880s.[16] Industrial activity, and the carbon revolution in particular, have therefore been a driver of inter-state cooperation, leading to measures such as the Convention on Long Range Transboundary Air Pollution (1983). More recently, the evidence that human action was leading to rapid and significant climate change led to the Paris Agreement (2015). It set global ambitions in response: to keep the average temperature increase below 2°C, and to 1.5°C if possible. This means, among other things, making sure that the peak in carbon release by human activity occurs as soon as possible.[17]

Disease is another dramatic example of the effects of natural and environmental factors: the plague, cholera, Spanish flu, HIV, SARS, and COVID-19 have all prompted collective action, at local, national, and international levels. This history of disease is considered in detail in the next chapter as an example of how changing organizational capacity allows more effective responses or creates the possibility for wholly new political ambitions to take hold.

Government and Technological Change

Techniques and technologies developed for economic purposes influence how collective institutions work, and how ambitiously they can be used, just as governmental techniques can be deployed for economic purposes.

This interaction can be illustrated through the history of data management. Writing was not a political invention. For centuries, in fact, it was associated with the Church, something reflected in our standard term 'clerk' (related to cleric) for someone who can record and handle written information. However, although it was not a governmental technology in origin, writing proved immensely useful for political organization. All sorts of rights and obligations were recorded in writing from the seventh century onwards, leading to an increasing reliance on the written record rather than memory, and the consequent importance of retaining and preserving important documents.[18] We still have Domesday book, nearly 1,000 years after it was produced, and the National Archives are home to miles of shelves of information that was once helpful to government. For example, we know who was living in some parishes in England in the 1270s because their tax liability was recorded and preserved in the remarkable hundred rolls. It was true too of local life: records of manorial courts survive from hundreds of years ago because what was written down was of such critical importance. The management of the British empire from its very beginnings depended on this management of information: written charters authorizing monopoly trading rights, the relay of diplomatic and other information essential to government, public debate about company privilege, political economy and strategy, accurate commercial information, and attempts to encourage native populations to engage with the stated ideals and ambitions of empire.[19] Much of what we take for granted about collective institutions rests on this technology.

Print, too, began as a private enterprise but was quickly adopted by governments. Very soon after the arrival of moveable type in England government sought to control what was circulating in print and to use print to make its own case. Simple techniques were adopted in handling government information: John Pym, a Somerset gentleman active as a local officeholder and MP, was an early adopter of the printed form in collecting royal revenues in the westcountry during the 1630s. By the late seventeenth century print was common in local government and during the eighteenth century the poor law administration was a major client for England's printers.[20] The advent of radio, television, and the internet in the twentieth century all created similar opportunities for government to collect and store information, and to disseminate its messages. Similarly, double-entry book-keeping, a technique used by Italian merchants from the late thirteenth century onwards, was eventually to be adopted by monarchs to help keep track of royal finance. The same is true for transport technologies (think of aviation, for example) or credit techniques (as we will see in the next chapter).

Changing technological capacity therefore helps to explain changing governmental ambition. For example, vaccination had been pioneered by a country doctor, Edward Jenner, in the 1790s as a way of dealing with the threat of cowpox. This created a new possibility for collective action, but that potential depended on institutional development. By the 1870s local Health Boards had acquired the power to try to ensure the vaccination of children, and this generated heated debate. The powers of Health Boards were part of a much wider revolution in government. In 1851 a national census was undertaken, producing a reliable record not just of how many people there were, but also their name, age, sex, marital status, place and date of birth, relationship to the head of household, and occupation. The territory itself was also being closely mapped by the Ordnance Survey. First deployed in the Scottish Highlands following the Jacobite rising in the mid-eighteenth century, this desire to know the lay of the land had a clearly military purpose: it was, after all, the *ordnance* survey. It was extended to the southern coastal regions in the light of the threat of French invasion in the 1790s, although by the end of the Napoleonic Wars only one-third of England and Wales had been mapped. The process was complete by 1853, however.[21]

Information management and new technologies have allowed a much closer regulation of social life since the nineteenth century. We are free within a system of close management and monitoring—we have rights to education, health, and various benefits, but only by conforming to this system and its categories. The agency of individuals and groups is exercised within the structures of the state—the limits of agency, and of government power, are two parts of the same dialogue—and the space in which that dialogue takes place is partly set by technology.

This interest in technology has often been military. Warfare has been a key driver of institutional change over long periods of history. Military mobilization was central to Roman life as we have seen and it helps to define the nature of post-Roman institutions—the warrior band, dynastic kingdoms, and the feudal compact, for example. The relationship between organized violence and wider social and political organization was the subject of a classic study by Michael Howard, who traced phases in political history in relation to the changing technology and organization of warfare.[22] Edward I's wars are an oft-cited example of how military innovation drove political change: building the state-of-the-art castle at Conwy, for example, along with the associated town walls, took four years, and cost £15,000. It was simply the most spectacular of a string of castles along the Gwynedd coast, and was associated with major military operations. Edward's invading army in 1277 had consisted of 15,500 men (9,000 of them Welsh) and there was a further campaign five years later. The total cost of all the castles and military expeditions was upwards of £170,000. That is hard to convert into 2019 values[23] but such demands played a significant role in structuring political relations with the aristocracy and boroughs (major towns that had been granted powers of self-government), who had in the end to find these resources. Over the thirteenth century land taxes were augmented by taxes on personal wealth, and customs duties. Population growth, the expansion of trade, and urbanization underpinned the elaboration of government institutions and the increasing complexity of monarchical rule.

It is often said that the adoption of gunpowder weapons in the sixteenth and seventeenth centuries was similarly transformative, amounting in effect to a 'military revolution',[24] and the connection is easy to see in the twentieth century too. With some exaggeration but also with some insight, A. J. P. Taylor once claimed that before the outbreak of the First World War 'a sensible, law-abiding Englishman could pass through life and hardly notice the

Figure 8. Manufacture of Merlin aircraft engines, 1942

existence of the state, beyond the post office and policeman'. In the following century, defence and security have driven considerable growth of state power and regulation. Between the 1930s and the 1970s (by which time the UK's global strategic interests had contracted dramatically) government played a key role in promoting technological innovation and efficient industrial production. The relationship between collective institutions and technology works in both directions, in other words. A sizeable portion of the civil service was engaged in these activities, harnessing science and technology in order to prepare for the demands of twentieth-century warfare (Figure 8).[25]

*　*　*

War is often treated as a material factor like the weather—external or 'exogenous' to political life, impacting from outside. However, like the economy, disease, and the environment (and in fact the weather), warfare is more complex than that. All these things are shaped by human behaviour, or caused by it, and enabled by institutional arrangements: warfare, like all these other challenges, is shaped and produced by collective institutions. Political life is also intimately shaped by economic behaviour, but the opposite is also true: the economy, and the effects of economic behaviour, have never been an area of life separate from politics. British governments have, for example, at different times promoted and sought to ban the trade in both enslaved people and the consumption of opium. These material factors—economic behaviour, environmental and technological change—interact with collective institutions but also, like mobilizing ideas, act on a different geography from them. Life on Britain has never, in that sense, been self-contained: its history is sometimes parallel to, but often shared with, much larger parts of the globe.

4

ORGANIZATIONAL CAPACITY AND THE CHANGING LIMITS OF THE POSSIBLE

W hat can actually be done depends in part on what collective institutions are available to do it. Organizational capacity shapes political action, and changes in that capacity mark out broad phases of political history: new institutions are created which then take on larger and larger roles in coordinating collective power. As we have seen, that creates path dependency— what is possible is partly determined by existing institutions, and they reflect the contours of previous decisions and settlements. New collective institutions, though, make new things possible.

This chapter first considers how differing institutional capacity allowed more or less successful responses to natural disasters, using the example of plague and famine in the fourteenth and seventeenth centuries. It then illustrates how institutional change can facilitate economic change, firstly through the effect of Roman rule in stimulating economic change and then through the use of collective institutions to limit the detrimental effects of individual behaviour that is harmful at the aggregate level. The final section turns to the issue of path dependency, tracing how different institutional histories affected how very similar social problems were addressed in the kingdoms of Scotland and England: how a set of arrangements reached at one point in time in relation to one problem set patterns and limits in addressing different problems subsequently. In all these ways, these examples illustrate how institutional capacity is itself an independent factor in shaping collective life.

Collective Institutions, Famine, and Disease

A good example of this is the contrasting effect of harvest failure between the fourteenth and seventeenth centuries. The death rate from harvest failure in the earlier period was far higher than in the face of a similar scale of harvest failure three centuries later and a substantial part of this difference can be explained by changes in institutional capacity.

Between 1280 and 1325 adverse weather impacted heavily on the English population. Cores taken from the Greenland ice sheet, correlated with the evidence of tree rings and temperature conditions in the Atlantic, suggest this was a period of exceptionally heavy rainfall and storminess. Manorial rolls reveal falls both in the amount of grain being sown and the yield of grain per acre, as the effects of one bad harvest affected the next year and compounded the problem. The total fall in output was without parallel in the eight centuries for which data exists. These may have been more severe than the problems experienced 300 years later, when harvests were also very bad for a sustained period, from around 1580 to 1640. However, the effects in the earlier period were magnified by the absence of the capacity to do much about it.

In both cases the total population was around 5 million, but the death rates were spectacularly different. It is estimated that

400,000 to 500,000 died in the Great Famine of 1315–17, while the three worst years of the later period, 1595–7, saw 'only' 40,000 deaths. The shortages of the later period clearly proved far less lethal. This is unlikely to be because the climatic conditions, or harvest failures, were ten times worse in the earlier period: the reason for the contrast is at least partly institutional.[1]

In general, a bad harvest becomes famine for reasons beyond simple shortages of food. Local shortages can often be remedied through imports and there can also be a social redistribution— from rich to poor. This latter point is critical because in many famine situations people die because they cannot afford to buy food rather than simply because there is no food. In Amartya Sen's famous formulation, they lack the 'exchange entitlements' necessary to get food.[2] The loss of life arising from harvest failure in the past could be ameliorated by redistributing food geographically and socially—fundamentally a task for collective institutions, since the market (aggregate individual behaviour) is what created the exchange entitlement problem.

Fourteenth-century evidence suggests that market activities made the shortages much worse—grain was hoarded, and often sold in late spring and early summer, in order to drive prices up, and sales were restricted to relatively narrow and established networks. The Crown did attempt to limit exports, and bishops instructed priests to condemn hoarding, but it seems clear that harvest problems became a Great Famine partly for human reasons. Matters were made worse by the demands of war. Grain was diverted to support armies, notably those engaged in an Anglo-Scottish war, and the financial burden of warfare was not handled in such a way as to make life easier for the poorest and most vulnerable. Other evidence suggests that neither neighbourly nor official intervention did much to mitigate the effects of poor harvests: debts continued to be prosecuted, landholdings of those suffering were bought up by their richer neighbours, and there is no sign of pity for those falling into crime or, for example, having children outside marriage after failing to establish the necessary independence to marry.

There is a sharp contrast in almost all these areas with the seventeenth-century experience. Obviously, it is the people who have to buy food that are most at risk—those living in towns, and in the countryside those without land of their own. And, of course, in both cases, poverty increases 'harvest sensitivity'. In the seventeenth century much more effective measures were imposed to protect these groups: preventing the hoarding or movement of grain to get higher prices at the expense of the local poor, and imposing price controls. These had the blessing and formal sanction of central government, increasingly systematized in the 'Books of Orders' issued to local officials, and were critical in trying to limit the damage of high prices.

Implementation of these measures rested on the cooperation of the network of local officeholders which was much more elaborate than that of the early fourteenth century. The key local institution was no longer the manor (central to economic and social regulation in the fourteenth century but geographically too small to support any very ambitious redistribution). By the later period the critical powers were exercised at county level, and in the largest towns, and essential to their success was the cooperation of the 'middling sort' who found these officially sanctioned measures useful in tackling this collective problem. These governmental powers were reinforced by charity and a kind of 'social economy' which set expectations: local gentry acknowledged their obligation to their poor neighbours by selling grain at below the market price, giving charity, and being willing to pay formal poor rates. The ultimate purpose was often, it seems, to defend their own social position but the effect was almost certainly to reduce the death rate: the total number of people vulnerable to high food prices was much larger than the number who actually died of hunger.[3]

These conditions had simply not pertained 300 years earlier. There had been no comparably developed middling sort who, through local officeholding, were engaging with governmental powers to regulate local society. A key reason for the very sharp contrast in the scale of mortality between the two periods was this social change, but also the institutional change which gave the middling sort the collective capacity to act in the face of bad harvests.[4]

The same institutional changes also allowed for a more active, and probably more effective, response to bubonic plague. It is only a slight exaggeration to say that the primary response to the arrival of the Black Death in 1348–9 was prayer and atonement. Cumulatively, in the years after that, the disease carried off around one-third of the population, in town and countryside, with long-lasting effects on economy and social structure.

By the seventeenth century, however, national and local governments were able to impose much more control over the impact of the disease. While an outbreak of the plague was still dreadful, and the experience of living through (or dying in) one was deeply traumatic, the overall impact was more limited. An outbreak in 1563 carried off one-third of London's population, and there were five further major outbreaks up to 1625. In 1603 30,000 died, while that in 1625 carried off 40,000–50,000. The most famous plague of all, in 1665–6, killed 70,000. While it was appalling, this did not match the scale of mortality in the fourteenth century. As with the famine example, the contrast was probably only partly 'natural'. There may have been some biological change: that selection had produced a more resistant human population, or that the most virulent strains of the disease had killed themselves too, and this has been suggested as an explanation for the disappearance of the plague from England after 1665–6. It seems clear, however, that human bodies remain vulnerable to the disease. An outbreak in Yunnan in the 1850s spread to Canton and Hong Kong in the 1890s, and from there to British India, where millions died. The mitigation of its effects in seventeenth-century England therefore seems to have been at least partly due to collective action (Figure 9).[5]

That action concentrated on policies of isolation. Houses visited by the plague were shut up, funerals took place at night or not at all, and movement out of places infected with the disease was curtailed. These powers were draconian—houses were marked as infected and those suffering the disease might also be shut up in 'pest houses'. There was also genuine compassion and heroism, as that demonstrated by the patient and diligent Ralph Tailor, working through the summer of a plague outbreak in Newcastle during the 1630s to ensure that the dying could make their wills, often via the window of a house that was shut up.[6] Most famously of all, perhaps, the villagers of Eyam in Derbyshire cut themselves off from contact with the outside world after plague arrived. Between September and December 1665 forty-two people died and as deaths began to rise again in the early summer of 1666 the vicar, William Mompesson, imposed a quarantine. A further 220 people in the village died, but this probably saved lives in the

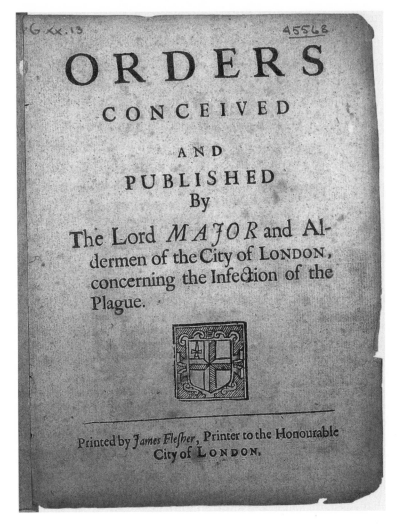

Figure 9. London plague orders, 1665

surrounding region—for four months from June onwards the village was cut off and the disease did not spread further.

This selflessness was reinforced by a weight of expectation that acted against the terror and desire to flee that many must have felt.

Although Mompesson's letters reveal an altruistic, self-sacrificing public spirit, they also show an awareness that those around Eyam expected the villagers to take such measures. The letters of the Hildyard family in Yorkshire reveal these expectations very clearly in relation to an outbreak of plague in Scarborough in 1598. Christopher Hildyard, a Justice of the Peace in the neighbouring East Riding of Yorkshire, had been reluctant to impose local rates to help the inhabitants in Scarborough on the grounds that the town should be looking after its own problems. His brother William had been outraged that the inhabitants of the town were allowing inhabitants to leave, reporting that Thomas Heddon had arrived at Preston in Holderness, 'very sore sick and unable neither to get up of his horse or ride'. He wrote 'you may see they deserve little at our hands that suffer their people so to endanger the country'. What had happened to Heddon, he added, 'as yet I do not hear'.[7]

The real transformation in collective agency in the face of the disease, of course, was the advent of pharmaceutical treatments. Plague is now easily treated with antibiotics. Although it is endemic in the Democratic Republic of Congo, Madagascar, and Peru, and present elsewhere, between 2010 and 2015 there were only 3,248 reported cases, of which 584 proved fatal.[8] Prior to that, institutions had helped limit the impact of the disease by effecting changes in behaviour. It is hard to be sure what the overall effect of these measures was but the incidence of the plague in the seventeenth century seems to have been less generalized, and overall mortality lower than in the fourteenth century, despite the fact that the population was more urbanized. Collective institutions seem to have offered a way to mitigate the effects of natural disaster. We have already seen how a similar capacity helped address the impact of cholera in nineteenth-century London, again in advance of effective medical treatment.

The modern impact of disease is far less dramatic as a result of advances in pharmaceutical science, but there is also an increased capacity to act collectively. This is another area in which interstate cooperation has delivered increased collective power. In 1948 the United Nations created a specialized agency, the World Health Organization (WHO), which has subsequently had a key coordinating role in leading the response to global health challenges— notably smallpox, malaria, Ebola, and HIV/AIDS. Like the plague, these diseases do not observe national borders, and although much of the success achieved in mitigating their effects reflects pharmaceutical science, behaviour change has also been very important. For example, the mortality rate associated with HIV/AIDS in many countries fell dramatically as a result of behaviour change before pharmaceutical breakthroughs had been achieved: the result of concerted attempts to inform the population about the disease and how it spread. The threat of diseases that are not (yet?) easily controlled using medicines is also met with concerted collective effort. The same is true of the response to perhaps the greatest threat of all—anti-microbial resistance. The WHO has led the development of action plans for individuals, policy makers, health care professionals, and farmers in relation to anti-biotic resistance which, by definition, is not currently controlled by pharmaceutical means.[9] Inter-governmental institutions have created the potential to take collective action at an international level in advance of any medical solution, just as superior collective power was available in the face of plague and famine in the seventeenth century as against the fourteenth century. One measure of the effectiveness of this organizational response is the success of the UK government's response to the 2009 outbreak of swine flu.[10]

At the time of writing it is too early to evaluate public responses to COVID-19 during 2020. No doubt subsequent analysis will show that some government strategies were more effective than others, but it seems that government action all around the globe reduced the death rate. That action was certainly dramatic: on 7 April 2020 the BBC reported that more than 100 governments had introduced some kind of lockdown.[11] It was estimated that up to one-third of the world's population was under such restrictions at the end of March 2020, and the effects on transport use and emissions were equally startling. This demonstration of the power of collective institutions though raised fears about individual liberty, and there were protests against these measures in many countries.

Secondly, although COVID-19 showed beyond all doubt that the great mobility of population and goods means that a public health problem in one part of the globe is a legitimate concern for the whole world, the WHO played a very limited role in coordinating international action. Moreover, COVID-19 is probably a symptom of an even larger issue: that of 'virus spillover' from other mammalian species. This is closely connected with local environmental and economic practices, and they can have catastrophic global effects. Coordinated and enforceable international action might well have reduced the death rate from COVID-19 even more, but that would require acceptance of a more effective global jurisdiction, as would any future regulation of environmental and economic activities to reduce the risks of virus spillover. While the WHO called for stricter regulation of wet markets globally in order to limit such risks, many commentators claimed that its investigation into the origins of the pandemic had enjoyed limited cooperation from the Chinese authorities. Meanwhile, it also had problems commanding support from the USA. Vaccination too is a global rather than simply domestic issue—no one is safe until everyone is safe. Again though, the WHO's global programme, COVAX, was under-funded, leading to calls for the G7 to step in to support it. Perhaps in response to these problems, some leading powers proposed addressing future pandemics through treaty agreements among sovereign states. These difficulties reflect exactly the same problems of striking a balance between collective and differential power, between national states claiming sovereignty and transnational organizations claiming jurisdiction, that bedevilled the UK's relationship with the EU.[12]

Promotion of public health through behaviour change has achieved significant domestic effects since 1948. The establishment of the NHS has created much more uniform standards of care, particularly between different social classes, but also great improvements in the capacity to change behaviour. Campaigns in favour of healthy eating and exercise, as well as against smoking and drinking, have had a significant impact on health and life expectancy. Some of these problems are not straightforwardly 'natural' but rather the result of forms of individual behaviour that have serious consequences in the longrun even though they do not seem obviously harmful as we experience them. Only collective education based on aggregate experience can prove the harm and encourage the change of behaviour. Again, this kind of effect is possible because of institutional structures—health organizations, local authorities, and national government agencies with responsibility for health. As we have seen, measures such as the Clean Air Acts have enormously improved our health, and in 2019 the Mayor of London led an initiative to create an ultra-low emissions zone in central London. It may not work but the important point here is that it is possible to try.

More powerful collective institutions have made a dramatic contribution to the extension of human life at a rate far exceeding any natural evolutionary change and on the basis of an essentially unchanged genetic inheritance. More generally, collective institutions have often mitigated the effects of disease long in advance of the availability of effective pharmaceutical treatments.

Collective Institutions and Economic Change:
The Romans

Organizational change can also drive economic change. For example, Roman institutional arrangements transformed the economic life of a large part of Great Britain. Prior to the Roman conquest much of the land had been cleared and there was already a developed agricultural economy, and the Romans had been drawn to the island by already existing trade connections, and by its wealth. In the period between the two Roman invasions land-holding seems to have consolidated and there was some development of specialized trades. For example, the quality of jewellery and some of the ceramics found in graves suggests that there was some trade specialization before the arrival of the Romans.

Nonetheless, despite the evidence that economic complexity was developing independently on Britain, the arrival of the Romans signalled a very rapid integration into a far more sophisticated economic world. The most dramatic illustration of this is the establishment of the island's first towns. Camulodunum (Colchester) and then Londinium were established as military supply ports, and a system of roads radiated out from Londinium which established a means to move both armies and commerce. By 100 Roman Britain had an impressive range of towns and cities, and the administrative centres hosted markets, law courts, urban amenities such as baths, theatre, and amphitheatres. All this promoted more sophisticated economic activity—the flourishing of specialized skills and trades. This was initially a direct product of the military presence and public spending centred on Rome, but it gave way in the second century to a more self-sustaining, provincialized economy.[13]

At Flag Fen the contrast is clear between the still visible line of the Roman road and the submerged timbers of the old causeway. The Roman road is a section of the Fen Causeway, which stretched nearly 25 miles eastwards from Peterborough, a spur of Ermine Street. Its course follows natural deposits of gravel over relatively high ground, but in other parts, as at Flag Fen, it is a human-made causeway across the Fen. Three phases of construction have been identified there. In the first phase the road was made of compacted gravel up to 10cm thick, bound together with wooden rods. A second phase laid a much thicker layer of gravel over it, again reinforced with wooden poles, forming a wider road—now 8m rather than the 5.6m of the first construction. The third phase produced a road twice as deep, 9.6m wide, which may also have had a cobbled surface. It seems to have had a primarily military purpose, and those phases of construction were attempts to overcome the liability to inundation. Above all, however, it reflects phases in administrative competence—the final phase apparently a product of administrative recovery in the late third or early fourth century after a period of governmental weakness. All phases, though, demonstrate the superior collective power at the disposal of Roman institutions, supporting a far more ambitious construction than the wooden causeway by its side.[14]

The very rapid growth of Londinium demonstrates how integration into the Roman military and political world produced almost instant economic complexity. Within twenty years of the conquest it was a highly developed port, home to soldiers, traders, officials, and migrants from across the empire. Summoned from nothing, like the nineteenth imperial cities of Melbourne or Adelaide, it offered opportunities without precedent on Great Britain.[15] The point is particularly clear if we compare the lowland south east of the island with the lowland belt of Scotland, which arguably had no towns before the twelfth century—more than a thousand years later—although there was clearly long-distance trade and consumption beyond the Romanized zone both before and after the arrival of the Romans. There are remains of large Iron Age hill forts in Scotland and evidence of accumulations of population at other central places, often with a military purpose, but none that satisfy a geographer's definition of a town—a place with specialized functions supporting a relatively dense population with clear occupational distinctions.[16]

If the arrival of the Romans had dramatic effects on economic behaviour, so too did their departure. Within forty years of the end of Roman rule urbanism was dead, large-scale artisan production had ceased, and in some areas the countryside had been abandoned. Luxury items disappear more or less altogether from the archaeological record and for 200 years all new buildings were of wood or dry-stone, with roofs of wood or thatch. The ability to build with masonry had simply disappeared. When Benedict Biscop, Abbot of Wearmouth, wanted to build churches in the Roman manner at the end of the seventh century—that is, with stone or brick and mortar—he had to bring artisans from Gaul, both those who could build with mortar and those who could glaze windows in the (elementary) style that he wanted. Literacy almost disappeared, and coins too.[17]

Over the following 400 years in the southeastern part of the island towns, crafts, and a landed aristocracy developed in close alliance with the development of royal power. Those kings increasingly looked to the continent for their models and inspiration, where Romanized forms of government had survived the fall of the empire more successfully. This illustrates very clearly how collective institutions frame economic possibilities. Changes in the fortune of Londinium could be emblematic here. By the eighth century London consisted of an ecclesiastical centre recently established within the Roman walls, and an undefended trading settlement established by the Anglo-Saxons outside the walls, at Aldwych and along the Strand.[18]

In Scotland the arrival of towns is closely associated with much later political action. Viking settlement in Scotland seems to have been primarily agricultural and it was not until the reign of David I (1124–53) that urban life came to Scotland. David had created two burghs, at Roxburgh and Berwick, before he came to the throne. They had a military function but were certainly intended to promote trade—they had market privileges and foreign merchants were prominent among their populations. By the end of his reign there were at eighteen such places, and by the end of the century thirty-eight royal burghs, and a further eighteen established by subordinate powers. Really, they were trading colonies with high populations of foreign merchants.[19] Clearly, collective institutions can promote new forms of economic behaviour and foster economic complexity.

The regulation of credit

The regulation of credit and debt gives another powerful demonstration of how collective institutions shape economic behaviour. Most of us depend on credit—we spend on credit cards before the money comes in to pay for the purchase, or we enjoy the benefit of a house or car while taking a long time actually to pay for it. It is even more essential to business'—money for stock or raw materials has to be paid out before goods can be manufactured or sold. Before the development of banks there were numerous ways around this, some of them highly unequal. For example, big merchants supplied raw materials to artisans which had to be manufactured and sold back to the merchant—'putting-out'—meaning that artisans had no real control over their work or its price. Those in these putting-out arrangements were often negotiating from a very weak position, in the absence of any other source of credit. On the other hand, other forms of credit were widespread, functional, and not exploitative: informal credit among peasants and small-producers or traders has been shown to have been an essential and positive form of economic behaviour in the fourteenth century as well as between the sixteenth and eighteenth centuries.[20]

In England and Scotland much credit was interpersonal—people carried round with them complex mental calculations about who owed them what, and these credit relations often had a strong personal dimension. During the eighteenth century these chains of credit became longer, more complex, and less personal, while the primary means of enforcing them was through locking debtors up. This created something of an epidemic of imprisonment that was potentially very damaging for commerce, since the prisoner might be subject to a run on their credit, and in any case was in a weaker position to try to make the money to pay their debts. Imprisonment was in that sense entirely counter-productive. Reform in the nineteenth century gradually overcame this, allowing merchants and the wealthier sort to declare bankruptcy, and limiting imprisonment to those who could pay but were unwilling to do so. At the same time, the rise of retail banking was eventually to mean that credit relationships were overwhelmingly between individuals and an institution rather than between individuals.

The rise of mortgages and commercial credit—now essential to the lives of most ordinary Britons—is not a natural or neutral economic development, therefore, but an institutionally structured one. For example, the Consumer Credit Act of 1974 had tried to make credit more freely available but had also imposed a tight regulatory framework. When this was removed in 1982 the effects on consumer credit were dramatic. At that point there were about 12 million credit or charge cards in use—enough for one each for about a quarter of the adult population. That had doubled by 1988 and by 2014 59 million cards were in use. The outstanding debt on these cards was £10 bn in 1993 and reached £57 bn by 2013. There was a similar boom in mortgage lending. In 1982 loans were characteristically capped at 80 per cent of the property value and limited to 2.5 times the borrower's annual income. By 1988 90 per cent or 100 per cent mortgages were common, and the borrowing limit had risen to four times the borrower's annual income. At that point home equity loans reached the equivalent of 4 per cent of GDP. By 2007 household debt was on average 1.6 times annual income. This boom in personal credit reflected a meeting between an appetite for borrowing and the commercial opportunity for those supplying the credit, and the removal of a collective restraint on both.[21]

Regulation of credit is now an international issue, since money moves so freely beyond national borders. The global consequences of licensing the trade in Credit Default Swaps (CDS) offer a dramatic illustration of this. A CDS involved allowing someone with a debt that might not be paid to swap it with someone else who was more optimistic, more able to bear the risk, or even more pessimistic about the debts they were already owed. It allowed the risk of bad debts to be shared and in so doing fuelled lending. In particular, it allowed banks to lend more. They were required to hold deposits equivalent to 8 per cent of their lending in order to cover bad debts, but they could now sell the risk. If the risk of the debt was held by someone else, the proportion of debt in relation to their deposits fell and they could resume lending. The CDS created three-way relationships like this. They originated in a large liability held by the bank JP Morgan from Exxon, arising from the major spillage from one of its tankers, the Exxon Valdez. Morgan swapped the risk of Exxon defaulting on its debt with the European Bank for Reconstruction and Development (EBRD) in return for a fee. It was thereby free to lend elsewhere, Exxon retained its line of credit, and the EBRD took on a risk in return for a fee. All three parties knew each other, and what risk they were taking on.

This kind of arrangement accelerated dramatically when such arrangements were 'securitized': bundled up together into a single investment. The idea was that a group of such arrangements could not all go bad. Investors were taking on a mixed bag of risk but were safe to take it on as a bundle. JP Morgan could keep swapping risk, and therefore continue to lend, while investors got returns on the good debts in the bundle but carried the risk of default on the bad ones. Even set out at this level of simplification, it is clear that this is far from a natural or inevitable way of doing business.

In fact, it evolved partly in response to previous forms of regulation: the constraints imposed on lending to restrain the effects of our apparently more or less unlimited individual appetite for borrowing. In order to be traded, this form of credit had to be licensed but it should not have been—it turned out that the statistical assurance that debts would not default on a dangerous scale was not good enough. The practice freed up lending that proved reckless because conventional views of risk had been dramatically revised; debtors defaulted, the availability of credit and some banks collapsed, and the effects were felt globally.[22]

These events are often presented as being beyond human agency, the outcome of the 'market', but we know when, where, and by whom securitized CDSs were invented, and when and by whom they were approved for sale. Neither of these things was inevitable. Financial products can be withheld from sale, at least potentially, no less easily than unusually polluting cars or hallucinogenic drugs.

There is a parallel story about the creation of the legal corporation, which trades in a regulated way that, for example, a crime family does not. It allows for credit, trade, and profit, but at the same time imposes the limits within which that can be done, taking account of the collective interest. In the later middle ages, when English merchants wanted to enter into long-distance, risky trades, they could form a regulated company. The Crown granted a monopoly on the trade, guaranteeing a return on comparatively risky investment, in return for services of various kinds. In the seventeenth century it became possible for groups to pool investment in return for a share of the profit—for example, putting up a percentage share of the cost of a voyage in return for the same percentage share of the profits. This spread the risk, making it manageable for individuals, and this allowed very risky and expensive enterprises to be attempted.

As we have seen, this greatly facilitated the expansion of the slave trade, underpinning the larger Atlantic system from which the UK profited enormously. Chartered and joint-stock companies were political and legal institutions that allowed new economic activity.

The joint-stock principle was greatly extended by the Companies Act of 1844 which made it possible to incorporate without royal or parliamentary approval, and legislation in 1855 introduced limits on the liability of individual shareholders for losses. The result was the modern corporation—treated in law as a legal person, whose shareholders take the profit but are insulated from total ruin if there are losses.[23] This has been good for investment and growth but less good at making corporations answerable for their actions.

Economic life does not simply shape collective institutions, then, but institutional arrangements allow economic activity to flourish. In contemporary political debate regulation is usually presented as a restraint and market activity as something that occurs naturally in the absence of such restraint. On any long-term view, though, we can see that production, distribution, and exchange are facilitated by, and do not simply facilitate, institutional life. We saw in Chapter 3 that collective institutions offer defences against free-riders and the harmful effects on the environment of individual actions. They also offer the only plausible defences against economic behaviour such as the individual appetite for borrowing which if unchecked can be highly destructive in aggregate.

Path Dependency

Collective institutions allow us greater control over the world around us—our institutional inheritance is a key factor affecting our capacity to control the social and material world. That is itself a product of history—agreements about collective power reached and institutionalized for one purpose create the institutional environment in which future collective action is shaped. Institutions and organizational techniques, once established, provide a resource for people trying to act in the future.

For example, Justices of the Peace (JPs) and village constables, so important to the responses to the plague and famine in England during the sixteenth and seventeenth centuries, were offices originally established for quite different purposes. During the late thirteenth and early fourteenth centuries English kings had offered royal justice to their subjects through Commissions of Oyer and Terminer—giving judges the power to hear and determine legal cases outside London. This became regularized in the circuits made by Assize Judges twice per year. As this new judicial apparatus became available, it attracted further business so that pretty soon Commissions of the Peace were created in each county, which met every three months to dispense justice in the name of the Crown: the Quarter Sessions. Only the most serious business now went to Assizes and Commissions of Oyer and Terminer became exceptional means to deal with emergency situations.[24] By the sixteenth century the Commissions of the Peace, consisting of the JPs, and regular Quarter Sessions were an established feature of local life. Their work was supported by High Constables, responsible for divisions of a county, and Petty Constables in each village. There was a parallel system in large towns which had been given borough charters.

By then, other potential uses were being found for this system and these local offices had become means of administration too. During the sixteenth century the number of pieces of legislation imposing responsibilities on JPs and constables grew from 130 to over 300—the so-called 'stacks of statutes' under which, according to one contemporary observer, these men laboured. These offices were critical, for example, to the assessment of the newest and most important parliamentary tax—the subsidy—as well as to the enforcement of religious change. It was they, not the Church Courts, who monitored church attendance and led the prosecution of religious opponents of the Crown as traitors (not heretics).

They also played a critical role in coping with the rapidly escalating problems of poverty and disease. Created as a means to bring royal justice to the localities, they had become an administrative tool of use in maintaining social order more generally. In that respect they might act with the general blessing of central government, and in the spirit of its directives, but with ambition and imagination of more local origin. In Dorchester, for example, following a fire in 1613, magistrates made a concerted effort to eradicate sin in order to assuage God's anger—this was, in the words of an influential preacher, a 'fire from heaven', sent to bring an erring people back to God. One measure of the success of the uses they made of their power was a drop in illegitimacy rates from above average levels to about half the national average during the 1620s and a quarter of the average in the following decade. Fathers and mothers were punished, and it seems that this resulted in actual changes in sexual behaviour. Such a local campaign was possible because of the existence of local institutions originally established for very different purposes.[25]

That ambition for social discipline was equally evident in Scotland in the same period but was expressed through quite different institutions. As we saw in Chapter 2, the reformation had come to Scotland through an aristocratic coup. Bishops had not brought Protestantism to the country and so the Protestant reformers greatly reduced their powers. Superintendents were introduced to strengthen the pastoral work of the Church and oversight of the whole structure was given (more or less) to the General Assembly. Parochial matters were given over to Kirk Sessions. These local bodies became (if they had not originally been) a vehicle for local initiative and they were very active in social regulation. The health of the local community—including matters of routine morality—were a matter for the Kirk Sessions, and so too matters of charity such as care for the poor.

The contrast is not absolute: in England the Church Courts also had a role in these matters of local morality, imposing shaming punishments that were quite effective in regulating personal conduct, while in Scotland secular courts were also active. Nonetheless, in the face of similar tasks and challenges, initiatives in neighbouring kingdoms were expressed through different institutions—one largely secular, the other closely linked to the Church. The distinctive origin of the Scottish reformation created the Kirk Sessions, which shaped not just the evolution of the Scottish Church but also patterns of social regulation.

Path dependency is also a way of understanding why the effects of the opening of transatlantic trade varied between different kingdoms. When European merchants began routinely to sail between the shores of Europe, Africa, and the Americas it created opportunities, but how those opportunities presented themselves to Europeans varied across the continent. Some of that, of course, was to do with geography—they were much more easily seized from the Atlantic coast than from the Alpine interior. Moving early also delivered a huge advantage—Spain and Portugal were able to stake very large international claims as first movers, although the mercantile activity that had first opened up these opportunities had not been simply Spanish or Portuguese.

What became of the opportunity therefore varied among European kingdoms because of the circumstances in which they encountered it. This point is perhaps best appreciated as a counterfactual. If (as is possible) Columbus had entered the service of Henry VII of England rather than Ferdinand and Isabella of Spain, England might have had access to South American silver and gold. Henry VIII would have been the richest monarch in Christendom, leading a major missionary effort in which Thomas More could have been a major figure. Papal support for the annulment of his marriage to Catherine of Aragon might have been lubricated by large donations, and Henry may have remained an opponent of the reformation, or Defender of the Faith (a title the Pope did actually give him in 1521). Money would also have delivered the military power to fully subjugate and incorporate the Irish, who would not now have been separated from the English by religion. It might also have allowed the English to recover and retain their lost territories in south-west France. In other words, if England had entered the Atlantic expansion earlier, it might have established its empire based on precious metals in the Caribbean and South America, rather than sugar and cotton in territories further north. The path of its social and political development would have been very different as a result.[26]

Path dependency is critical in understanding the differing experience of shared or parallel global developments. We have seen, for example, how in the nineteenth century European capital was seeking returns in increasingly global markets, and that for the British this was associated with formal empire while in the US it was expressed in westward expansion. This had further contrasting effects when global depression spread during the 1930s. There was a strong desire to promote growth through free trade, but protectionist policies won out everywhere. In the US investment for growth turned inwards but in the UK was associated with a policy of Imperial Tariff Preferences, seeking to promote growth by tying the economies of the empire more closely together. This was led by a Conservative government, reversing a commitment to free trade made with painful consequences for the party in the mid-nineteenth century. In effect the prime minister, Neville Chamberlain, had to introduce tariffs in order to then give preferential treatment to the British colonies. This relationship with the formal empire was also critical to the experience of post-war reconstruction, complicating the approach to European economic and political cooperation while at the same time adding to the sense of post-war malaise as decolonization accelerated. None of these circumstances was unique to Britain, but the experience of them was shaped by the institutional inheritance—by the legacy of arrangements made in quite different circumstances for different purposes.

*　*　*

Institutional factors affect what can be made of an opportunity and how to deal with a challenge. Institutions created for one reason offer the means to tackle later, quite different, issues—and can prove helpful or limiting in that later context. Possibilities in the present and the future are shaped by the inheritance of the past: the accumulation of past decisions and resolutions created an institutional inheritance through which we experience the present and address the future. This institutional inheritance provides part of the environment in which people act. It is a significant part of what people have to work with (or against) when addressing collective problems or acting on new ideas; and new institutions create new possibilities.

5

GEOGRAPHIES OF COLLECTIVE INSTITUTIONS AND IDENTITIES

Which Groups Take Action for What Purposes?

Great Britain has not always been an island. The BBC once reported news of research on the last time the sea cut the connection with the rest of Europe under the headline 'The moment Britain became an island',[1] but of course, at that point, no one knew it was Britain. The question posed in this chapter is something more like 'when did this island become Britain, for what purposes, and for how long?'.

Over the long run people have acted at larger and smaller scales, and in doing so have formed collective solidarities other than those of Britishness. This is one reason why a concentration on the origins of the UK and British national identity gives such a partial impression of political history. This chapter considers these varying geographies of collective institutions and identities, outlining the enduring importance of local and regional structures and identities, then of the dynastic and national structures of kingdoms and states, and then of international and supra national bodies. The final section of the chapter considers some of the complexity of the relationships between these institutions and identities.

The essential point, though, is that institutions, identities, and political action have rarely mapped onto the island—they have operated at larger and smaller scales and connected Great Britain with other parts of Europe and the world. There is no historical evidence to suggest that it is naturally a self-contained or self-sufficient political community. However, we need to balance awareness of that fact with the equally undeniable fact that path dependency has created the UK and British citizenship, which now powerfully shape the lives and consciousnesses of its inhabitants.

Local and Regional Structures

Some fascinating written sources survive from Roman Britain that reveal the everyday concerns of ordinary people. There are inscriptions, as well as writing tablets that survived in the thick mud of the river Walbrook (now buried under London) and at the fort at Vindolanda, and on the 'curse tablets' left at the Roman baths in Bath. These sources capture a world of familiar local and personal concerns—worries about supplies of food, beer, and clothes; the behaviour of a local military commander; and, famously, a birthday party invitation. The Vindolanda tablets reveal a slang term for the Britons in use among the Roman soldiers, as well as notes about military tactics and behaviour. Behind that presumably lies a sense of Roman-ness, but in these sources that was taken for granted, and was certainly not routinely stated. What mattered instead was the local task in hand. The 130 curse tablets found at Bath were appeals to the goddess Sulis Minerva to intervene in cases of theft. For example, one placed by Docimedis, who had lost a pair of gloves, asked that the perpetrator 'lose his minds [sic] and eyes'. In that context the identities in play are not so much Roman and Briton as thief and victim. While it makes sense to write the history of Rome, therefore, it can also make sense to write a history for the same lives which makes little reference to that over-arching identity.

For much of the period covered by this book many people lived their lives around local institutions and rhythms. The Anglo-Saxon law codes, and the role of local assemblies in enforcing them, reveal the importance of the regulation of ordinary life, of course—restitution for wrongs and defence against injustice. The importance of these local structures is reflected too in the coinage—usually seen as one of the key markers of royal authority. The location of the mints in the tenth and eleventh centuries, however, does not seem to reflect practicality or the pattern of royal power—rather the pattern of local administrative arrangements and rights. While abbots and lords were not represented on the coins, their interests shaped where and how the coins were made, and hence how royal projects were made to work.[2]

After the Norman conquest of England these political and tenurial relationships were codified systematically—lords offered service to the Crown in return for land. They extracted service from their tenants—particularly the duty to work a certain number of days on certain tasks for the Lord, and to pay agreed fines (fees) and rents. Tenants, because they were unfree, were subject to the authority of the manor court and did not have access to royal courts; but on the other hand, they had some influence over proceedings in those manor courts.

The economic shocks of the fourteenth century—famine and disease—greatly improved the bargaining position of the peasants, speeding the decline of serfdom, and local lordship was increasingly displaced by the local institutions of royal government. There had been public courts since the Anglo-Saxon period, but they now loomed larger (at least potentially) in the lives of ordinary people alongside the Lord's manorial courts. Quickening trade created new opportunities in urban markets, and towns could increasingly deal directly with the Crown. Urban charters and liberties again ceded a large degree of local control in return for agreed services to the king. Local government grew in close association with the institutions of the Church— the parish church but also religious houses. These English institutional arrangements were extended to Wales in 1535 and 1542 (which also made English the official language of government).

This was the origin of a system of government subsequently known to historians as 'self-government at the king's command'— subjects acknowledged the rights of the Crown but were also able to use royal power to run their own affairs. We saw in Chapter 4 how the elaboration of these local institutions by the seventeenth century enabled much more purposeful action in the face of plague and harvest failure. In England and Wales the maintenance of roads and bridges, for example, was a shared responsibility of this largely autonomous system of local government—national legislation enabled but did not enforce these measures. New functions were added to these institutions continuously. For example, churchwardens acquired responsibility for pest control during the sixteenth century. They already had responsibility for maintaining the fabric of the church but new legislation to protect grain put them in charge of paying out bounties for the killing of 'nuisance' animals—birds, hedgehogs, badgers, and so on. Between local common law courts, the manor court, and the local church, many aspects of local life were regulated with little need to engage with larger institutions or shared identities; their deliberations were not very far removed from ordinary people.

There were similar developments in lowland Scotland, although the extent of urbanization and formal institutionalization of these relationships was more limited, and local lordship seems to have been important for longer. We have seen how the reformation in Scotland created a relatively decentralized Church structure, in which local congregations had some autonomy, and that included matters of moral regulation. Those institutions often provided a more ready means to act than the local institutions of royal government, which were less well developed than those in England.

Such institutions provide a powerful basis for local identities. For example, in England, the rights and powers of borough governments were marked in civic ritual that was often tied to the religious calendar. The feast of Corpus Christi was from the fourteenth century onwards a regular feature of urban life, each urban guild playing a particular role in the processions and entertainments, the various groups within the town coming together as a whole social body. The regular circuit of the Assize Judges was another such moment, marked with pomp and ceremony, while Quarter Sessions added to the hustle and bustle of the regular life of market towns. These rights and jurisdictions generated shared experiences that underpinned a collective identity. Local churches recorded local history and belonging: the gifts of local benefactors, the tombs of important local figures, and representations of biblical stories and teaching that were distinctive to the parish and could be a source of emotional attachment. In a sense these memorials and decorations created a local church from the universal one. Roger Martin, a churchwarden in Long Melford, Suffolk, in the period of the reformation, recorded in loving detail the decoration and local rituals attached to his church as they were being swept away by Protestant reform. An opponent of the changes, his description reveals the profound sense of loss he felt, both as a matter of local pride and belonging as well as of theological critique.[3]

These rituals marked out the year throughout Christendom, but distinctive traditions focused on local identities. At Bury St Edmunds, for example, on St Edmund's day, a white bull was led through the town. Married women who had not had children walked alongside it, stroking its flanks as they processed towards the precincts of the abbey. This was clearly a fertility ritual of highly individual significance, but also a ceremony of collective local belonging—an experience which all the inhabitants of Bury shared and which distinguished them from the inhabitants of other towns. The annual agricultural cycle was also marked by regular local ritual tied to religious feast days, again a focus for local solidarity and belonging.[4]

Historians of sixteenth- and seventeenth-century England have placed great weight on the importance of these local, county, and regional identities. Gentry families tended to marry within the county, and compete for influence over county institutions, and through that lens England could appear almost a federation of semi-autonomous county communities. Larger cultural provinces have been identified too, held together by patterns of production and exchange, inter-marriage, and collective institutions. Such solidarities might prove difficult for royal government to break into—even in 1589, the Armada year when a concerted

Spanish invasion attempt was underway, it proved difficult to get the Yorkshire gentry to meet their formal obligations in relation to national defence. This can be, and in fact has been, over-stated: ordinary people engaged with national courts, paid national taxes, and consumed national and international news during this period. However, there is no doubt that for many collective purposes local, county, and regional institutions were sufficient.

Of course, local authority could be just as authoritarian and restrictive as central authority. A perennial question about any collective identity is 'who is *not* included?'. This is the subject of Chapter 6, but it is worth noting here that 'local' does not necessarily mean 'inclusive'. As the English poor law developed, parishes acquired clearer responsibilities for dealing with poverty, and it became important to establish which parish had responsibility for which pauper. Where children were involved this could lead to scenes of some brutality—mothers being questioned in labour about who the father was (pain was assumed to bring out the truth in a society which had only recently given up on torture), and there are stories of women in labour being moved over parish boundaries as people tried to avoid having to take responsibility for the child. The 'settlement laws' sought to regulate who was responsible for whom, and during the eighteenth century amounted to an ambitious social discipline.[5]

During the nineteenth century rural self-government was weakened by the proliferation of centralizing measures—the older institutions of local government lost ground to professionalized services such as the police and public health boards. In other ways, though, it was a heroic period for local government action, particularly in the major cities. Urban government was reformed to meet the needs of rapidly growing population and these newly

Figure 10. Glasgow City Chambers

empowered civic bodies provided a framework for ambitious local action. This public collective action was supplemented by equally ambitious programmes of philanthropy. This too was associated with considerable local pride, as in Birmingham's memory of Joseph Chamberlain and his municipal socialism. Those who led social improvement in Glasgow, pursuing measures similar to Chamberlain's in Birmingham, have left unmistakable marks of civic pride and belonging in the city (Figure 10).[6]

Again, however, there were social boundaries to these civic communities. There was, for example, evidence of some scepticism among the Sheffield working class about the value of their new university in the early twentieth century: one 'Strutter', a skilled engineer interviewed in the course of a social survey, told the interviewer (as several others had done) how the workers had been asked to subscribe to the university and 'laughed at the idea that it was of any use to the workers'.[7]

In the late twentieth century there was a concerted attempt to limit these local powers—local authorities were seen in Westminster as rivals or impediments, using their taxing and spending powers to subvert or challenge the priorities of national government. The poll tax of the 1980s was introduced partly because of the weaknesses of the previous system of financing local government through local rates. However, while there was a clear need to reform the rates, an issue which successive governments had dodged, there was also a clearly political element in this attempt to clip the wings of local authorities.[8]

These pressures on the powers of local authorities have exerted a sustained effect, but local identities and local institutions have been very durable and powerful over the long run. In recent years the reduction in the powers of local authorities has been offset by other initiatives—attempts to create the capacity for coordinated regional economic action (the Local Enterprise Partnerships or, for example, the plan for a Northern Powerhouse), or elected mayors, for example. In principle such local authorities could still answer many of our collective needs and can be a means to coordinate responses to challenges operating over much larger scales too. For example, they are the best means to try to regulate recycling schemes and a powerful tool in responding to climate change by discouraging the use of cars.

Dynastic and National Structures

Countless historical accounts have made the history of national institutions familiar—they have provided justice, raised taxes, or provided the arena of political ambition and ideological conflict.

There are numerous examples too of national legislation achieving positive social effects—the amelioration of the effects of poverty, the reduction of road deaths, improvement of air quality, provision of free education and health care, and so on. Equally, in histories of popular politics, the battle to bend the will of national government is familiar—for example, in the histories of franchise reform or civil rights. There is therefore no need to emphasize how important national institutions have been.

What is less familiar, perhaps, is the varying geography of these 'national' states. At no point in the period covered by this book has the island been both an integrated political community *and* self-contained. Collective institutions have controlled either parts of the island, or the island as well as territories elsewhere. That has reflected the geography of dynastic and imperial politics, not simply national identities or community.

The kingdoms of the post-Roman era occupied small territories, largely but not entirely confined to Great Britain: the kingdom of the Dalriada straddled the Irish Sea. The 'Other England' formed by Viking settlement was ruled between Dublin and York before the West Saxons conquered Viking territory on what became the English part of Great Britain. Some of these kingdoms had long lives—Wessex, for example, lasted four centuries, although its institutions and identity are now largely lost. The ambitions of these kingdoms did not naturally extend to the shores of the island—for example, the construction of Offa's Dyke, however mysterious it remains, seems to mark the limits of Mercian territorial ambition in the west and is obviously well within the bounds of the island. On the other hand, as they developed, these kingdoms pursued dynastic interests that took their rule beyond the island or brought them within the rule of dynasties based elsewhere. The Orkneys, for example, were under Norwegian rule or overlordship for even longer than Wessex lasted.

Wessex became the core of an English kingdom under the pressure of resistance to Viking expansion. Subsequent conquest by descendants of the Vikings who had settled in northern France drew the interests of the English Crown south and west, creating cross-channel dynastic interests that embroiled kings of England in war and diplomacy in France—eventually creating powerful interests in the rich wine and salt regions of south-west France in particular. There was a security problem for them in the north and west, which was to lead to invasions of Wales and Scotland in the thirteenth century, but the legacy of the Norman conquest was a set of dynastic claims and economic interests that drew the English kingdom into the dynastic politics of France. Only slowly did the language of the court become English, and more slowly still did the eyes of kings in England settle on the north and west.

So, although it is often said with some justification that the Kingdom of England was a precociously centralized and uniform national state, its borders have not been stable. Those borders reflected the dynastic interests of the ruler rather than the national identity of the people—which is why the Kingdom of England is a less familiar term than, say, the Norman or Angevin Kingdom. The extension of its authority to roughly the borders with what became the Kingdom of Scotland and Principality of Wales was an achievement of the tenth century, but it was only catastrophic losses in the Hundred Years' War during the fifteenth century that decisively severed connections with the continent. Even then, of course, the dynastic authority of the king of England was not limited to England, or to a part of Great Britain. The creation of a Kingdom of Ireland in 1542, under the authority of the king of

England, took their political interests to the neighbouring island and, by the early seventeenth century, the establishment of English colonies extended their interests across the Atlantic.

The Kingdom of Scotland was centred in the lowland belt but before the sixteenth century the rest of modern Scotland was only poorly integrated into its orbit or was actually subject to other authorities. In fact, the earlier strengthening of the Kingdoms of England and Scotland may actually have led to greater problems in asserting their authority at the margins—the borders, highlands, and islands.[9] Diplomatic relations at that point drew the Scottish political elite into French politics, which created at least some chance that Scotland could for a time have become a French rather than British territory.

In the eleventh century Gruffydd ap Llywelyn had ruled a large part of what is now Wales, and there was an organic development of political life in directions similar to those in England. The Welsh principality, however, was founded during the thirteenth century by Llywelyn the Great who extended his authority from Gwynedd in the north to the south and east. In doing so he acknowledged fealty to King Henry III of England in the Treaty of Worcester (1218), and the regularization of his government of the principality was related to the need to make regular payments to the English Crown. At the end of the century frictions with Edward I led Llywelyn the Great's grandson, Llywelyn ap Gruffydd, to refuse to pay homage to the English King. The result was conquest, the introduction of the English common law, and the construction of a string of castles along the coast of Llywelyn's Gwynedd heartland. The statute of Rhuddlan (1284) annexed the principality to England and made it the endowment of the heir to the English throne. As we have seen, after the 1530s the principality was absorbed fully into the English

Crown, acquiring counties and the pattern of law and administration associated with them. It is hard to separate the creation of a unified Welsh principality from the exercise of English jurisdiction, therefore, despite the undoubted reality of Welsh identity.

Many of these dynastic kingdoms had relatively short histories within shifting borders that did not straightforwardly reflect a shared national interest among those subject to them. The British state, which succeeded the Kingdoms of England and Scotland, also has a much shorter and more complex history than is sometimes appreciated. There are two key issues here: firstly, the creation of the United Kingdom and, secondly, its definition as a national state, answerable to citizens who identified themselves as British. This rests on parliamentary sovereignty—that the ultimate power in the state is vested in a representative body. Both these features of the modern UK emerged from the complex events of the seventeenth century.

The crowns of Scotland and England (which brought with it the Kingdom of Ireland) were united in 1603, the result of dynastic calculations about succession to the throne. The first king to hold both crowns, James VI and I (1567–1625 in Scotland, 1603–25 in England), wanted to govern a Great Britain, but the difficulty of managing three quite different realms was no small part of the causes of what became a crisis of Three Kingdoms during the reign of his son, Charles I (1625–49). What emerged was forged in the contingencies of war and revolution, not the vision of a monarch.

In Scotland Charles I was seen as a threat to the true Protestant religion. The political community united around a National Covenant in order to defend the religious settlement from an unreliable king, eventually raising an army to make their point. This caused cracks to open in the English kingdom, further exacerbated by a rebellion in Ireland in 1641. There Protestantism had failed to take hold, and reliable Protestants had been settled there to defend royal authority. This drove a wedge not just between Protestant settlers and their tenants and those they displaced, but also between them and Gaelic elites who felt their power eroding. Charles I seemed to many Irish Catholics a source of protection from a bigoted Westminster parliament. Disastrously for Charles, the rebels in Ireland claimed they had his support, so that the English parliament would not trust their king with an army to deal with the Irish rebellion. The combined effect of these crises was the total collapse of royal authority in both England and Scotland, and the resulting war was incredibly destructive and expensive.

In England it led to administrative revolution, and eventually a peace settlement achieved by executing Charles I and abolishing the monarchy along with the House of Lords and Church of England: the English revolution. The English then defended their settlement using their newly acquired military might, leading to the conquest of Ireland and a temporary conquest of Scotland. When the Stuart monarchy was restored in 1660 Charles II (1660–85) found this financial and military power very helpful, and more or less accepted the permanent presence of parliaments which it required. This relationship was cemented in the decade after the Glorious Revolution of 1689, which saw the military and financial power of the state hiked again, and the creation of a national debt in which tens of thousands of investors had a direct interest. England was by now a major player in European expansion around the globe, and that helped tempt the Scots to join a fuller union in 1707. Scotland was represented in the Westminster parliament, although it retained a separate church and legal system.

That union created a British state but was also fundamentally an imperial project, giving Scots access to an expanding empire: it was not in any obvious way a national union of all the British on the island and no one else. At that point, in fact, around 250,000 British subjects lived in its American colonies (the population of England and Wales was around 5 million). The loss of thirteen colonies in 1776 did not prevent a rapid expansion of British imperial power during the first three-quarters of the nineteenth century—military and political dominance was underpinned by an unchallenged position as workshop of the world. The extension of British power in India and then Africa, the growth of the colonies of Australia and New Zealand, as well as settlement and trading domination in south-east Asia created a truly global imperial state. Britain and its empire formed at the same time, in other words. A shared British identity was fostered, often consciously, in support of these institutional arrangements—it is not at all clear that the institutions built on a powerful desire to express a shared Britishness.

Finally, in 1801 Ireland was brought into the United Kingdom of Great Britain and Ireland, losing its (at least supposedly) independent institutions, and formally extending the British state beyond Great Britain. In 1921 the independence of the southern part of the island of Ireland was confirmed, leaving the UK covering all of Britain and part of the neighbouring island.

If we were to sum this up, then, at no point before 1707 was Great Britain a single political entity. At that point, though, when it was unified, its authority also extended well beyond the island—to Ireland but also in a developing imperial system. The establishment of an independent Irish republic left part of that island within the UK. Considered in these strictly geographical terms,

Great Britain has never been both a unified *and* self-contained political entity.

The development of parliamentary sovereignty was no less messy, but again the mid-seventeenth-century crisis was critical to it. In the course of the civil war and its aftermath parliament had taken hold of financial and military power within what remained a dynastic agglomerate. That Charles II got Bombay and Tangier as part of the deal when he married Catherine of Braganza in 1662 indicates how these dynastic politics co-existed with the development of maritime empires. Opponents of the regime could continue to press their opposition by promoting alternative claimants to the throne as they had done throughout the period of the dynastic kingdoms—for the Old and Young Pretenders who raised armies to claim the throne in 1715 and 1745.

Nonetheless, monarchs were eventually to be eclipsed by parliaments. Wars were increasingly justified as matters of national, not dynastic interest—the extension of diplomacy intended to foster trade and settlement. Most significantly, though, executive power migrated into parliament. During the eighteenth century the key minister became the person who could command a majority in parliament—the prime minister—not the person who dominated the politics of court and royal council. Governments were formed within parliament by a majority of MPs. Rather than parliament advising, then balancing and restraining the executive power of the monarch, the electorate and MPs now hold the executive to account *within* parliament. MPs from the majority party form both the basis of executive authority—in that their leader is the prime minister—and the majority of the people's representatives, responsible for restraining and scrutinizing the actions of that executive. This is a complex and sometimes messy set of arrangements, which in the early stages of the Johnson government in 2019 seemed to many people to make little sense. Other states, such as France and the USA, in which executive monarchies were replaced in conscious revolutions that constructed alternative constitutional arrangements, have a much clearer separation of powers.

The UK and its sovereign parliament are both therefore products of an accumulating institutional inheritance, of particular decisions taken in specific circumstances, rather than the outcome of a planned or natural evolution, nor are they an expression of a strong prior political identity.

Supra-national and Inter-State Organizations

There is a very long history connecting the collective institutions on Great Britain with wider territories. In part this is the product of political ambition— for example, the encounter with the Romans, and with Norwegians in Scotland and Danes and Normans in England; or the dynastic interests of the Angevins and Plantagenets. At the same time, the inhabitants of the Kingdoms of Scotland and England were all members of a much wider Catholic Church in the early sixteenth century, while they made common cause over subsequent religious and secular arguments with fellow travellers across Europe and the globe—Calvinism, communism, neo-liberalism, and environmentalism, for example.

During the twentieth century, however, the scale of international institutional cooperation increased. We have seen how the Westphalian system expanded at Versailles and how the

League of Nations attempted to bring more order and equity to the international order, while international economic stability was promoted through the gold standard and attempts to foster monetary stability following the stock market crash of 1929. In the post-war period, however, there was a much more sustained ambition to foster a global economic order underpinned by a systematic view of political economy. The UN, NATO, and Warsaw Pact were more coherent versions of the state system as it had evolved from the mid-seventeenth century, but they were associated with rival views too of the economic and social order. There was global cooperation to rebuild European and Japanese economies in particular, and a broader recognition of economic interdependence.

Cold War competition was a significant element of the need (as the Western powers saw it) to combat the growth of international communism as a solution to these problems. Security and stability would be assured through a global political economy, which would foster a desirable political order. In the West this was a model of liberal democracy, underpinned by market economics, steady growth, and modest redistribution of wealth. There was formal and informal inter-state cooperation to promote these ends. It had a rival, of course, in the Soviet bloc fostering centralized economies and much more ambitious programmes of redistribution. The competition took the form of a race for growth and the achievement of other desirable hallmarks of modern success—putting men on the moon, or men and women on the Olympic medal winners' rostrum, for example.

Inter-state organizations, although often effective in managing global problems, are often sclerotic and always open to criticism for lack of genuine representative legitimacy. Citizens are represented via their national governments, and often decision-making is fundamentally shaped by the interests of the most powerful states. The UN Security Council, of which the post-war nuclear powers are permanent members, is notoriously frequently dead-locked. These inter-state organizations have proved indispensable in their ability to coordinate collective power, but their differential power seems to many ordinary citizens immune to influence.

At the extreme end of dissatisfaction with such bodies are the conspiracy theories about a world order operating behind these organizations in which national governments are at best dupes. But transnational and global politics have fostered a more active response too: ideological solidarities across national boundaries aimed at influencing these collective insti-tutions. Nineteenth-century communists often argued that for the revolution to prosper it would have to be global in reach, and the successive communist internationals sought to coord-inate the development of socialist politics transnationally. In the twentieth century volunteers from across Europe signed up for the international brigades in the Spanish civil war, seeing in that war a conflict of significance for everyone, not just the Spanish. Basque refugee children were given homes in camps across the UK: an expression of international ideological soli-darity and humanitarian concern. Transnational and inter-state co-cooperation since that time have fostered a similarly more ambitious range of civil movements: the Campaign for Nuclear Disarmament or movements for civil rights and environmental action, for example (Figure 11).

A consequence of this is that many of our active transnational identities are partisan or ideological, rather than that of a people. At one time, people across much of Western Europe were connected by their membership of the Western Church and bound into a

Figure 11. Anti-apartheid protest, Cardiff, 1969

collective identity as members of Christendom. The reformation fractured that identity as Christians became increasingly aware of what divided them, but at the same time encounters in Africa and America created a sharper sense of a shared European identity, defined in terms of biology, as well as political and social assumptions. There was no European empire, though: there were rival European powers each creating their own, so that there was no single collective institution through which Europeanness was even theoretically expressed. By contrast, the UK speaks for a nation (or claims to) and answers to the British for its actions. There is a shared identity underpinning NATO, the UN, and the World Bank and other transnational organizations and Iriye has argued that such governmental and non-governmental international organizations are creating a sense of global community. However, there is no direct way of bringing collective pressure to bear on those institutions and other commentators argue that the democratization of global governance, and the range of interest to which global institutions respond, needs to improve rapidly.[10] Where we organize internationally it is usually less as citizens of the world than as a people with a shared partisan aim, organized as a single-issue lobby (and often with a very weak voice).

This has been crucial for the politics of the EU, which originated as an inter-state organization, coordinating production and trade. Its structure reflects that but, as we have seen, grafted onto it are functions that seem more than that. The demands of a single market have created concomitant demands for regulation and economic management, including the free movement of labour, fostering resentment of a body that is really fitted for inter-state negotiation rather than for democratic governance. But these transnational and supranational institutions respond to the logic of political action—global economic and political challenges requiring collective action have driven their development. As the Brexit negotiations revealed, there are many functions that people are very happy to see carried out at European level—notably security.

As in other areas of political life, inter-state and transnational cooperation has been mirrored by transnational mobilization outside institutions, intended to put pressure on them to behave in a particular way, or to limit the scope of their action. That creates ideological identities that reach across the globe, and which cut against an attempt to restrict political action to the country of citizenship. However, that has not so far created collective identities meaningfully and directly expressed through those other collective institutions.

Institutions, People, and Political Identities

All these institutions—Mercia, the Kingdom of Scotland, the UK—developed under their own logic, and were not simply the natural expression of primordial or all-encompassing identities. In fact, collective identities are formed by, as much as they form, collective institutions.

For example, a sense of Englishness can be traced to King Alfred's court, where it gained currency in the face of the collective threat posed by Viking invasion: we might see Englishness becoming more meaningful in the face of a functional challenge. A British identity embracing all of Scotland and Wales gained more traction following the eighteenth-century union, and was associated with the growth of a British empire.[11] In both cases there was an institutional focus, but in the ninth century English institutions were a product rather than a cause of the political usefulness of the shared identity; the eighteenth-century example suggests more that the identity followed from the success of the institution. Moreover, that British identity was clearly 'nested' with other national identities—English, Irish, Scottish, and Welsh (and, in some eyes, Cornish).

Collective identity has often been deliberately fostered in order to strengthen institutions. The earliest example we have seen is Agricola's attempt to do this in the Roman Province. New forms of royal ceremony in the nineteenth century were similarly intended to cement loyalty to the British Crown, in this case against the background of rapid industrialization and urbanization. From the 1870s onwards there was a concerted attempt to use ceremonial to enhance the dignity and regality of the monarch, supported by the national press, and the greater ease of movement to witness these great ceremonial events. At the start of Victoria's reign many commentators thought royal ceremonial in the UK was by European standards poorly developed and received with pretty limited reverence. By the end of her reign it had changed. Her successor's coronation was described quite differently: 'For the first time in the history of our land, did the Imperial idea blaze forth into prominence, as the sons and daughters of the Empire gathered together from the ends of the earth to take their part. The archaic traditions of the Middle Ages were enlarged in their scope so as to include the modern splendour of a mighty empire.' The appeal to the past was explicitly linked here to the novelty of this ceremonial—a mix memorably summarized as the invention of tradition.[12]

The success of such nation-building efforts is not always clear. There is continuing debate about how far claims of loyalty to king and country were actually credible in the First World War, although the eagerness with which many men signed up suggests that they had more power than post-war critics had suggested. However, National Service after the Second World War, intended not simply as a way to meet the functional needs of the British military but also to foster a national civic culture, did not seem to perform either function particularly well. Certainly, the memories and memoirs of national service are full of stories of the solidarities it created, but they are not framed in terms of national patriotism.[13] Rather, many national servicemen seem to have developed a profound and shared suspicion of the claims of the national establishment.

There has also of course been a continuing diversity of identities on Great Britain. Britishness was not achieved at the expense of local political action, for example. The Westminster parliament which stood at the heart of the empire was, like the dynastic monarchy before it, an important resource for those trying to achieve more local purposes. A strong tradition of local government was maintained in the eighteenth and nineteenth centuries, and as parliament became a permanent partner, it developed as an institution that facilitated as much as it directed local life. Private legislation—prompted by local lobbies—formed the bulk of law making, creating the possibility of local and regional action on a scale not possible through manor and borough courts, or JPs. This embraced Scotland and Wales too, of course.[14]

These collective identities rarely embrace all the inhabitants of a territory either. In fact, in claiming authority in the name of a people some states have not only failed to act for all of the people within a territory but have actively created racial and ethnic exclusions. Territory and people are never perfectly matched: not everyone within a territory necessarily feels the force of the shared identity equally or in the same way (as with Scottish or Black Britons, for example) and may in fact be regarded as a member of another group (as with recent migrants, for example). Subjects or citizens from ethnic-minority backgrounds have often faced formal and informal exclusions—Jews in the medieval period, or those who had migrated from the Caribbean up to and including the Windrush scandal of 2018. So too have temporary migrants and refugees, from French or Dutch Protestants in the period of the reformation to East European workers from the EU in the years before the 2016 referendum.

Modern nationalists therefore tend to speak of a civic rather than ethnic patriotism—the pride they foster is in the institution rather than the ethnic identity, the qualities of the state rather than the people. What is great about the UK in other words is not skin colour or DNA, but the institutions of UK government. Many advocates of Scottish independence are very keen to make this distinction—that it is a civic not an ethnic nationalism. By contrast, a major failing of attachment to the EU among those who voted for Brexit seems to have been exactly this: pride in the institutions and collective achievement of the EU was not felt by many British citizens (it had not after all been promoted by British politicians over the previous forty years). It is therefore ironic, but also revealing, that the Brexit debate was presented and understood as an issue in identity politics as much as a discussion about how to get things done. People were identified not as having expressed an opinion about the practical value and prospects of the EU so much as their personal identity: Brexiteer or Remainer; as being from a tribe of somewheres or anywheres.[15]

Drawing attention to the (so far) fairly brief histories of kingdoms with their current boundaries, or of British identity, is not intended to deny the reality of these identities in the twenty-first century, or the plausibility of independent and sovereign states based around them. It is simply to point out that they are not self-evidently natural arrangements, or a natural way of being that has been lost, nor do they in themselves solve the problem of deciding what needs to be done or how to do it, or who gets to act. They are complicated by more local or by ideological solidarities, by issues of inclusion and exclusion, and also by their relationship with a much wider set of interests in the former British empire and elsewhere.

* * *

Returning to the question posed at the beginning of the chapter, the island became Britain between the fourteenth and seventeenth centuries, in a process of dynastic agglomeration rather than national self-realization. Over the long run people on Great Britain have made their lives in overarching institutional structures created by dynastic ambition, chance, and military conquest, and more recently at second-hand through inter-state and transnational organizations. Different collective ambitions have been expressed at different geographical scales—local, regional, national, and international. Many different identities have been mobilized, or forged, in order to achieve collective ends—Mancunian, Lancastrian, English, British, fascist, and vegan. Institutions have never had a monopoly on collective interests or an unchallenged claim on particular individuals, therefore—most people have been able to express a shared interest and seek influence through a number of collective institutions. Rather than a single community, there have at any one time been multiple, overlapping political communities, each of which was potentially itself divided. Geography, collective institutions, and identities have never neatly mapped onto one another. In the strictest sense, then, Great Britain has not been a political community very often or for very long—people have operated at smaller and larger scales for particular purposes throughout the recorded history, and before that.

On the other hand, institutional structures create shared interests, and can therefore foster a shared identity. How a group of people encounter the world is shaped by their collective institutions, and what they can do about it is likewise connected to this collective identity. It would therefore be foolish to deny the reality or importance of modern national identities—English, Welsh, Scottish, or British. Path dependency has created UK citizens who often feel more than one 'national' identity and those citizens encounter the world through membership of inter-state and supra-state organizations—UN, NATO, and the common-wealth. They do so, though, on terms set by their UK citizenship. Recognizing the role of path dependency is not to deny the reality of the institutions and identities with which we currently live, but to understand better how patterns have been set and, by implication, how they might be re-set for the future. We act through the UK, but we may also act at other levels and with potentially greater effect.

Taking the long view reveals how identities vary considerably over time. It is possible to find English identity in the ninth century, but others, equally important then, now seem to mean little—Mercian or Norse, for example. National institutions and identities have clearly been important to political life, but these 'nations' have also varied widely in extent. Above all, this tangled history demonstrates that to take a pattern of institutions and political identities as they stand at one moment—the current place of Westminster and Britishness, for example—and project that into the past gives only a partial view of that past. That matters. If an understanding of the past helps us to make sense of the present and to imagine the future, then it follows that a partial view of the past is profoundly limiting for the political imagination.

6

POLITICAL INCLUSION

Who Makes Things Happen?

How effectively do collective institutions reflect the interests they claim to serve? Clearly, they can reinforce or create differential power, entrenching vested interests, but can also limit inequalities. Which effect they have is fundamentally related to who gets to make them act.

A conventional history of Britain and Britishness puts the development of the UK and of representative democracy at the centre of the story. On that view the agency of ordinary people has steadily increased as their representative national body—parliament—acquired power and then came to respond more directly to their views through the ballot box. That is, of course, a very important aspect of British history, but it is only a partial view of how people have used collective institutions to exercise control over their social and material world. As we have seen, they have acted in all sorts of ways and at other geographical scales. This is significant because there is a powerful feeling across many contemporary democracies that the ballot box is not enough, that it does not deliver real agency—broadening our understanding of how agency has been expressed in the past is helpful in thinking about that problem.

This chapter first outlines forms of inequality before discussing techniques by which ordinary people have accessed, first, the power of ideas and, second, the power of institutions. Overall, this provides a deeper historical context for the agency delivered by mass representative democracy and its limits, and the fourth section of the chapter offers some brief reflections on that. The final section considers some weaker forms of agency, and how they can be a source of opportunity, dignity, and recognition even if they fall short of the power actually to significantly affect the workings of collective institutions.

Inequality: Differential Power

There are many sources of inequality. Most obviously, the control of the important commodities in any society—trade goods, land, or money, for example—gives some people or groups more power than others. The uses made of collective institutions has always been connected to the interests of elite groups—from the great landholding magnates of the medieval period to the industrialists and financiers of the more recent past.

However, such material things are not the only ones that matter to society. How society is understood gives more value to some people than others—men, white people, heterosexuals, and older people have all been empowered by assumptions about what the natural order should look like, and by their power to speak for it or to act as its guardians. The power that follows from speaking for religious and supernatural beliefs, and from defining or controlling access to such deeper truths, is also an apparently universal feature of human society. In fact, inequalities like this are used to explain the archaeological record, even where there is no archaeological evidence to support the interpretation. Thus, the druidical elite said to have regulated access to Stonehenge is a matter of pure speculation which is persuasive in part because it seems like common sense.

At least from the Roman period on we can be sure that social, legal, economic, and political arrangements have systematically empowered men more than women, reflecting deeper assumptions about gender difference. This is not to say that all men were more powerful than all women—most men who have lived on Great Britain had access to less power than Boudica, Elizabeth I, or J. K. Rowling. Nonetheless, overall, the ways people are empowered, and the limits on that, are gendered. Those gendered limits have often been reinforced by formal political and legal exclusions—from property rights, access to education, voting rights, and equal pay.

We do not need to look far for the formalization of racial, ethnic, and religious exclusions either. Accumulating prejudice and hostility to the Jews resulted in their exclusion from England in the thirteenth century, only partially remedied by their readmission in the mid-seventeenth, while the informal exclusion of Jewish people from the political establishment persisted well into the twentieth. Following the reformation, Roman Catholics eventually became a minority in England, barred from public office between the seventeenth and the early nineteenth centuries and, again, subject to informal exclusion long after that. From very early in English history the Irish were regarded as 'wild', and from the sixteenth century this was reinforced by religious difference. During the English civil war (1642–1646) it was made illegal to accept the surrender of Irish troops fighting in England, on pain of death,[1] and by the mid-twentieth century a hostile stereotype was well ingrained. By then, it was associated with hostility to immigrants from the wider British empire—notoriously captured in the signs declaring 'No dogs, No Irish, No Blacks'.

Forms of unfreedom have also been persistent. There were enslaved people in England before the Roman conquest, Roman life was based on slavery, and forms of slavery persisted into the eleventh century. By then, formalized serfdom had become widespread, based on a form of land tenure—in holding a piece of land the serf accepted (was forced into) a legal relationship with very tight restrictions. The difference was in one way fundamental—slavery aims at denying rights, while serfdom charged for them, exacting labour and other services in return for rights to marriage, family life, and inheritance. Both can be seen, though, as variations on constantly evolving forms of 'unfreedom' that were imposed across Europe for millennia: there had been unfree tenants in the seventh century, and the full flourishing of serfdom took some time.[2] These 'base tenures' and their associated legal disadvantages were uncommon by 1450 but they nonetheless persisted into the sixteenth and even seventeenth century, although their practical consequences had been greatly reduced. During the English civil war, some parliamentarians claimed that the war was not simply against the Crown, but against slavery—for men like John Lilburne the enemy in the war was not Charles I but the tyranny that threatened to enslave freeborn Englishmen. There is some irony, then, that important men in that parliamentary coalition were at that very moment beginning to use indentured labour to establish colonies abroad and establishing a slave society on Barbados which created a blueprint for commercial empire, leading to the immiseration of millions of Africans. And if poor

Britons could claim formal legal equality, they did not have equal access to political power, of course. The right to formal political representation was limited by wealth well into the nineteenth century—in fact, against this long history of exclusion poor men have had the vote only slightly longer than women.

These inequalities reflect influential ideas about what holds society together. The place of the poor, women, and outsiders helps define the natural order and political power has often been used to protect those dominant visions. Hostility to outsiders is not simply a matter of protecting jobs and access to other resources, but hostility to what they represent. They pose a 'normative' threat: that is, they are thought to undermine principles on which a particular society is grounded because they live by different norms. Perhaps the clearest example of this kind of hostility, unrelated to any real competition over material resources, is exclusion based on sexuality. It is incredible to my children that homosexuality was illegal during my lifetime, and that men were actually imprisoned for it. Of course, as with all these other examples, the end of formal and legal sanctions did not end informal exclusions and the experience of prejudice.

There is no need to labour this obvious point, that collective institutions can entrench the power of those who are already powerful for some other reason. This might be directly true, in that political power is used to protect vested interests—economic, cultural, or ritual, for example. Or it might be true in a more subtle way, exerting an influence that moulds the response to an objective problem like poverty, disease, or a financial crash. For example, the poor laws in place from the sixteenth to the nineteenth centuries offered help but also imposed a social discipline on the poor, which was intended to protect the larger, unequal, social order. Class interests inflected the implementation of the Contagious Diseases Acts during the 1860s, which targeted not just the poor, but poor women specifically. Police powers to stop and search people on suspicion that they might be criminal (the 'Sus' laws) were notoriously liable to be a vehicle for racial prejudice and discrimination. They originated in vagrancy laws from the 1820s but their use in the 1970s was associated with racial profiling, and they were repealed in 1981. Governments have been tempted to reinstate similar laws since then, raising the same fears.[3]

However, there are ways that the relatively weak can take better control over their lives and prevent the use of collective institutions simply to protect powerful vested interests. The rest of this chapter offers a thematic view of how that has been done.

Accessing the Power of Ideas

Appropriation

Ideas used to justify political power can be manipulated in order to restrain government, or to force it to act. In academic language, this is known as 'appropriation': taking advantage of an argument used by powerful people or institutions to call them into action, or back to their supposed principles. It works by shaming them or threatening to expose them as hypocrites. Powerful people do not invent the ideas they use, or at least cannot control how they are commonly understood. Having appealed to a powerful idea, therefore, they can be influenced by how their audience chooses to understand it.[4] A queen who claims to be acting on God's behalf in effect submits her actions to a judgement: all her subjects can assess for themselves whether her behaviour is in fact godly. What is commonly understood to be good Christian behaviour can be used as a standard against which to judge how someone is actually behaving and to prompt them to take a particular action. Awareness of this potentially restrains the powerful.

For example, grain riots in the sixteenth and seventeenth centuries, far from being anguished and inchoate cries of pain, took advantage of official policy. Rioters halted shipments of grain to force a local sale. In some cases they took half the grain, leaving the other half for the Crown—effectively implementing at their own initiative official measures against profiteering which made half a seized shipment forfeit to the Crown and the other half available to the local poor. Grain rioters proclaimed through actions like this that they were not engaged in theft but were applying the price controls which local authorities had failed to impose. The point was to jog the authorities into action or to fill in for their neglect. In one sense, then, in making claims about fair prices and concern for the poor the government had offered a hostage to fortune.[5]

This appropriation is a common feature of political history. We can see it at work, for example, in a powerful speech delivered in Hartford, Connecticut in 1913 by Emmeline Pankhurst, a prominent campaigner for women's right to vote. She had already been imprisoned four times and fully expected to be in prison again on her return to the UK. Much of her famous speech is a justification for the confrontational tactics adopted by the Suffragettes, but the essential case rested on an appropriation of entirely conventional arguments: her fight, she said, was to win the rights of citizenship. She urged on the men in the audience 'the fact—a very simple fact—that women are human beings'. Appropriating the universalism of claims about citizenship, she asked what men had done when not able to claim their rights as citizens. It did not take a great leap of imagination for a New England audience to think what the American revolutionaries did with the idea that they were subject to taxation without representation. This was the war in which Emmeline saw herself as a soldier. While the behaviour and political tactics of the Suffragettes might seem shocking, Pankhurst said, they had been forced into it because they could not behave as citizens and expect to be heard (Figure 12).[6]

Speaking in Wolverhampton a few years later, in 1918, twelve days after the Armistice that ended the First World War, Lloyd George said that there was an obligation to make the UK 'a fit country for heroes to live in'. Real measures were taken to deliver on that aspiration: it led to the building of council houses, for

Figure 12. Emmeline Pankhurst speaking

example. However, the promise of a land fit for heroes also became a means to shame future governments. This flight of rhetoric justified many future claims on government attention, not least the hunger marches that punctuated the next fifteen years, and could be a powerful indictment of the hypocrisy of government that served the interests of the wealthy and powerful. It is easy to multiply such examples.

Triangulation

At no point in the period covered by this book has life on Britain been regulated by a single mobilizing idea. In the Anglo-Saxon period Christian ideas sat alongside values associated with kinship and lordship, Roman values and legal principles derived from Germanic sources. As we saw in Chapter 2, Simon De Montfort balanced ideas about his personal honour, Christian belief, good government, and obligations to the monarch in thinking about how to act. This complexity creates the possibility of playing off one set of values against another—of triangulating ideological claims.

For example, in 1614 James I of England imposed a 'benevolence': a rather Orwellian term for a gift demanded from his subjects which they could not refuse without being punished (a more accurate term might be a tax). Oliver St John, a trained and very able lawyer, does not count as an ordinary person, but he perhaps spoke for them when he resisted this. He claimed that by refusing to pay he was actually carrying out his duty as a subject to help the King: if the people were to pay, he said, they would be helping the King to break the law. In doing that, they faced 'a hellish danger since very irreligiously and uncharitably we help forward the King's Majesty in that grievous sin of perjury'.[7] In effect, he was playing off his obligation to help the monarch uphold his coronation oath against his duty as a subject to pay up when the monarch told him to.

Religious ideas have often proven powerful in this kind of triangulation. In January 1641 poor women from London jostled members of the aristocracy as they arrived and left the House of Lords, demanding that they agree to the permanent exclusion of the Bishops from the Lords. This was a remarkable event—people excluded from formal power by their class and gender demanding a fundamental constitutional change and acting without proper deference. They justified themselves by saying that parliament's failure to resolve the conflict was the result of a successful popish plot. This had resulted in an extended economic crisis which meant that they could not feed their children. While convention would not normally allow them an opinion on such a fundamental constitutional issue, it did allow them to call on their governors to act to help their children. This gave them the opportunity to voice a very radical idea—that Bishops were by their nature popish and should therefore be excluded from parliament, seen by these women as the guardian of Protestantism.[8]

Political influence has also often been linked to claims about social virtues, and these too have often been contested. A decline of deference in the UK over the last few decades reflects how alternative ideas of virtue undercut the claims of the wealthy, well-born, highly educated, and expert. Monty Python made something of a specialism out of satirizing the claims of the establishment, based on just this kind of triangulation—appealing to other kinds of virtue to show up the limitations of upper-class twits and government ministers. The pretensions of the powerful can be punctured by pointing to their human frailties—their unrestrained or unconventional sexual appetites or even bodily functions. Those with larger than normal 'animal appetites' are revealed to be lacking the higher virtues that they claim, and there is a long tradition of drawing attention to the private sins, embarrassing appetites, and personal failings of public figures (Figure 13).

Figure 13. Gillray, *The Voluptuary under the Horrors of Digestion,* 1792

Rejection, Subversion, and Imagining Alternative Worlds

Very strong ideological claims have often resulted, at least in the short-term, in a different form of agency. A useful academic term here is expressive recognition: being recognized as someone with a legitimate voice, even if the immediate effect of that voice is limited. Simon De Montfort, as we have seen, embraced a grisly death and thereby gave testimony to the sincerity of the political claims he had made. As John Lilburne put it in the mid-seventeenth century, 'though we fail our truths will prosper'. Such self-annihilating courage, while often of limited immediate effect, can exercise a latent force on politics, an implied threat, that restrains the powerful and sometimes wins future victories. This is the core of the martyrological tradition from Thomas Becket through the reformation period and, beginning in the mid-seventeenth century, it was secularized. It is a pattern of politics that can be traced, for example, via the Tolpuddle Martyrs (transported to Australia for organizing a labour union in the early nineteenth century) and the Suffragettes to the Irish republican hunger strikers of the early 1980s, who refused food unless they were recognized as political prisoners rather than criminals.

During the eighteenth century more humble people made a similar sort of claim, for less lofty purposes. Execution was a public spectacle, and the official hope was that the condemned would make a penitent end, acknowledging the justness of their execution, and thereby become advocates for the legal order they had broken. Many, though, chose instead to 'die game': that is, to go to their deaths with a swagger, and perhaps also with defiance. On one level this was a futile gesture—they were still executed—but they were apparently asserting a desire to be recognized as individuals, and the performance was often appreciated by the crowd.[9]

There is a very deep-rooted subversive tradition, for example in ideas of Christian egalitarianism that for centuries underpinned critiques of established powers. As the radical priest John Ball asked in 1381, 'when Adam delved and Eve span, who was then the gentleman?', a question that recurred in the English Revolution and later.[10] At other times too, millenarian movements promising the imminent arrival of a new society have had the potential to completely undercut established values. For example, in England in 1649–50, the Diggers founded a community based on a 'new law of righteousness', in which the community worked as a collective, and in which individual property and ambition was submerged in the collective service of God.

The appeal to alternative values was an important part of the various late medieval and early modern versions of the Robin Hood story—a group living outside the law who actually live by more admirable values than their governors. In some forms the story includes a wholly hypocritical friar—supposedly committed to a life of poverty in imitation of Christ, and dependent on the charity of ordinary believers, but in practice a drunk, a glutton, and a fighter who lived by theft. In these stories he is, nonetheless, to be admired. In one sense this might have a similar function to travel literature and ethnography. From Tacitus writing about Germania, to European observers of the rest of the globe in much later periods, such writing has often held a mirror up to conventional society—outlining the virtues and vices of other societies as a way of gaining perspective on one's own. This might lead to very radical reconsiderations of the value of accepted ways of life.

During the crisis of the mid-seventeenth century many radical new views about the basis of government were articulated in England—many people feared that this was a world turned upside down. It was not, but the 1640s and 1650s did see political partisanship emerge as a way of self-assertion for individuals and groups: a royalist soldier could challenge a parliamentarian gentleman by appealing to partisan values. From the nineteenth century onwards socialist and communist views have rejected established values no less comprehensively, and during the 1960s and 1970s communes flourished in many Western countries inspired by a rejection of bourgeois respectability and a quest for personal self-expression, partly informed by travel on the hippy trail and the assimilation of 'Eastern' belief and practice. Environmentalism offers fundamental challenges to standard views of the position of humans in relation to natural resources and other species. Individuals and groups can deploy new ideas, in other words, in the hope of shifting the use of collective institutions in radically new directions.

Accessing the Power of Collective Institutions

Lobbying and Petitioning

The power to act usually comes through existing collective institutions and there is a long history of trying to influence them. Relatively organized lobbies, established to do this, represent a form of action analogous to the appropriation of ideological resources: trying to make existing forms of power work in favour of a particular group.

Lobbying became increasingly visible and regularized as the growth of regal jurisdiction in the thirteenth century created various chartered bodies. For example, large towns were incorporated as boroughs and given powers of self-government alongside obligations to serve the Crown. As we have seen, groups of traders and merchants were given trading privileges and monopolies, again with an expectation of service to the Crown in return. These chartered bodies also acted as organized lobbies. Monarchs who promised justice could be petitioned by subjects who needed particular things done.

In the following centuries, the density of such institutions grew and royal authority was communicated more regularly and coherently to wider audiences, and this jurisdictional view of kingship was filled out by views of the common good. Governmental literacy, record keeping, and formal legislation underpinned a view that kings exercised authority on behalf of the whole realm through increasingly clearly defined jurisdictions. Earlier kings were seen as lords—offering protection and favour in return for loyalty and service in the same way that their followers did for those below them. Now kings claimed to exercise a different kind of authority in addition to this—on behalf of all their subjects. Thus, the king could issue writs *quo warranto*, demanding to know by what legal right this or that thing was being done. It was also associated with formal taxation for the public good—that the king could raise taxes for the good of the realm, since the good of the realm was something that touched all his subjects. Finally, it was associated with the codification of the English common law. These developments were a feature of the politics of the kingdom of Scotland too.[11] All this offered a hostage to fortune for future monarchs.

From the fourteenth century onwards towns, counties, guilds, and merchant corporations made formal representation to kings and parliaments in petitions which called on governors to redress wrongs, do justice, or live up to their account of themselves. 'Taxation boroughs' had higher tax obligations but also therefore a stronger claim on royal attention. It became normal from 1295 onwards for boroughs to be directly represented in parliament, and the number of borough MPs continued to expand thereafter. There was another phase of expansion between 1500 and 1640 when the number of boroughs in England increased from 38 to 181, in Wales from 3 to 14, and in Scotland from 35 to 58. This enabled local action (for example, in relation to poverty, famine, and plague) but also more organized representations to royal government. Boroughs themselves were similarly pressured by organized lobbies. They regulated commercial activities by monitoring weights, measures, and prices, and enforcing communal morality. The differing interests of occupational groups were institutionalized in guilds, enforcing commercial regulation and craft rules.

Petitioning was accelerated by the advent of printing. During the 1640s, when press controls had collapsed, and parliament was in permanent session, petitions circulated widely and not just to the body being petitioned. Putting together a petitioning campaign became a way of building support and not just expressing a grievance. More than this, people began to sign petitions as individuals who shared an ideological position, rather than as members of a corporate body, such as a town or guild. For example, the Levellers petitioned on the basis that a political settlement after the sufferings of the civil war would require an *Agreement of the People*—they were petitioning in the name of all those interested in protecting the common freedom of the people, rather than those sharing, for example, an interest in soap manufacture.

Urbanization during the nineteenth century, the concentration of labour in large factories, and the continued development of mass communication made this kind of collective mobilization ever more powerful. Campaigns for franchise reform—the Chartists, Suffragists, and Suffragettes—and twentieth-century social movements—the Campaign for Nuclear Disarmament, for example—were able to mobilize ideological communities to pressure the institutions of government.

One way historians talk about this is as a product of diversifying forms of 'civil society' or 'associational life'—that is, the possibilities for social interaction with others on the basis of shared values and beliefs rather than of simple neighbourhood. A ninth-century village had few spaces for social life, and a small and relatively undifferentiated population. Eighteenth- and nineteenth-century towns had much greater and more diverse possibilities, creating a social environment in which Friendly Societies, Corresponding Societies, Trades Unions, and eventually Non-Governmental Organizations could thrive. They in turn could address their concerns to increasingly powerful national institutions.

Communication technology has been an important factor in this. Just as print allowed the transformation of petitioning, for conversations to take place which would have otherwise been impossible and the formation of ideological bonds over large distances, so have more recent changes in communication. In the ideal, such free expression allows for the rational consideration of political virtues and possibilities, but the liberation of print from pre-publication licensing during the seventeenth century immediately led to anxiety about the quality of public discussion—whether it was in fact rational, courteous, and wel informed was highly questionable. The same set of possibilities and anxieties have been unleashed by new social media, of course.

Collective mobilizations hold a mirror to particular sets of institutions—for each political institution there is now the possibility of a sphere of critical commentary in which its strengths and weaknesses are debated. From Sheffield Council to the G7, different organized interests come together to reflect critically on the conduct of institutions, and to apply pressure to them.

Triangulation: Using the Law and the Church

It is often possible to play one institution off against another, as with the triangulation of ideas and values. In fact, the pretext for the Claudian invasion of Britain in AD 43 fits this pattern: native leaders appealed to Rome for protection from their local rivals. In effect, those threatened by the expansion of Catuvellauni territory under Caratacus had been able to appeal to another source of power for help.

The stability of dynastic kingdoms was often threatened by the possibility of appealing to alternative claimants to the succession. Following the death of William the Conqueror, in 1087, his lands were divided, leading to further invasion and civil war during the reign of Henry I. This was fuelled not just by the ambitions of the protagonists but also the political calculations made by the aristocracy, who chose sides according to which claim favoured their own interests. A similar opportunity was presented when Richard I died in 1199, leaving no male heir. His brother John's claim to the throne was supported by barons in England and Normandy, and by his mother, who controlled Aquitaine. The claim of his nephew, Arthur of Brittany, however, was supported by barons in Anjou, Maine, and Touraine. John's problems were exacerbated by conflict with the Papacy over the appointment of the Archbishop of Canterbury in 1205, leading the Pope first to suspend religious ceremonies in England for five years and then, in 1209, to excommunicate the king.

The power of alternative claimants to disturb political order was a recurring feature of dynastic politics in the kingdoms both of Scotland and England through, for example, the Wars of the Roses, the claims to the English throne of Lambert Simnel and Perkin Warbeck which gathered support during the 1480s and 1490s, the turbulence in Scotland in the sixteenth century, and the claims of the Stuart Pretenders in the eighteenth century. Each one offered at least some people the chance to improve their fortunes by changing the monarch. In 1685 the succession of the Catholic James II to his older brother's throne in England prompted the Duke of Monmouth to mount a rival claim. Monmouth was Charles II's illegitimate son, and so was not a perfect candidate, but he had the great advantage of being a Protestant in an overwhelmingly Protestant country. He did not only have God on his side, though—he was supported by a plebeian army made up of people who saw in this rival claim an opportunity.[12]

As we have seen, during the thirteenth century royal government became increasingly formalized and this shaped how royal power was challenged and harnessed. It is one way of thinking about Magna Carta in 1215, signed as a formal resolution to King John's problems with his barons and the Papacy. It had an uncertain start as a guarantee of liberty, but among other things it stated that there would in future be no taxation without consent.

Henry III was later forced to submit to regular parliamentary sessions in order to negotiate his power, and this is one reason why the history of parliament is conventionally traced to this agreement. Magna Carta is a symptom of the way that detailed formal agreements framed the exercise of differential power. We saw in Chapter 2 how Henry faced his own baronial rebellion forty years later, and in the course of those disputes he too agreed to more formal restraints and answered for his conduct to parliament.

The formalization of government and codification of the common law thereafter restrained monarchs and government and could be an important source of agency. Between 1500 and 1640 there was a rapid increase in litigation in central courts, fed by prosperity and the growth of the legal profession—at that point there was probably more litigation per head of population in England than at any other time in history. This is often seen by historians as a sign of social strain, but it can be seen more positively: that more people had ready access to the law than at any other time. The historian who discovered this grew up in Maryland in the era of the civil rights campaigns, and was very conscious of the virtue of ready access to the law on equal terms for all citizens.[13] Much of it was interpersonal, rather than between governors and governed, and involved debt and commercial arrangements rather than political liberty, but from the fifteenth century onwards ordinary people found the law a useful tool. It was also a defence against tyranny. Radicals like John Lilburne in the 1640s or John Wilkes in the 1760s were protected by juries from prosecution for what they had written, and during the 1790s, in the shadow of the French revolution, a number of attempts to prosecute radical writers for 'seditious libel' failed, despite the evident intentions of the government and leading judges.[14]

The institutions of the Church, and not just religious ideas, have also offered a way to offset or challenge the powerful. For example, the era of reformation politics created opportunities for agency, as generations of English Catholics claimed that by taking the English Church back into the arms of Rome, they were seeking to save English government from itself, or to reclaim it from the hands of those who were leading England to spiritual ruin. In Scotland, the reformation became a way to yoke the power of the king, diluting Crown control of the Church and thereby creating a potentially rival source of power in the kingdom.

In regions where institutional power is weak or contested, individuals or groups have often had greater leverage. The border between England and Scotland, for example, created opportunities for cattle thieves between the fourteenth and sixteenth centuries— they could cross the border, take cattle, and then escape beyond the reach of the law by crossing back. Neither the English nor Scottish crowns could offer secure protection, and so instead local tenants were given their land on favourable terms in return for military service. In the Elizabethan period the whole of the north of England was treated as a special case, with special powers, under the Council of the North, just as those areas bordering on Wales were under a Council of the Marches. When Scotland and England were united under the same king in 1603 the border disappeared, and with it both the threats and opportunities it had created.[15]

Similarly, opportunities were available at the margins of British imperial power, and the high point of empire meant that UK governments were anxious to assert their power in distant places. In 1847 the house of David Pacifico was attacked by an anti-Semitic crowd in Athens. The police observed the attack but did not intervene, and Pacifico suffered considerable damage to his property.

The crowd had been incensed, it seems, by the banning of the tradition of hanging Judas Escariot in effigy at Easter—the government had banned it in order to avoid giving offence to the banker Mayer de Rothschild, who was due to visit and from whom the government hoped to secure helpful loans. Pacifico, also known as Don Pacifico, had been Portuguese Consul General and was a leading figure in the local Jewish community. It was as a British subject, however, that he sought redress. Back in London this became the focus for a debate about the justness of Palmerston's foreign policy, which was marked by the use of threats and gun boat diplomacy. In the course of those debates Pacifico's rights were compared to those of a Roman—captured in the famous phrase *civis romanus sum* (I am a Roman citizen), a statement that (if true) was sufficient to secure the safety of any individual travelling across the Roman empire. Don Pacifico, in claiming his rights as a British subject, was said to be equally free from indignity and the UK government gave its support to his claims for compensation.[16]

Contested succession, the institutions of the law and the Church, and rival jurisdictions at the margins of political territory have all provided opportunities for triangulation between collective institutions, creating the possibility of political agency.

Alternatives to Existing Institutions: Direct Action

The period between the Peasant Revolt in 1381 and Kett's Rebellion in 1549 was the great age of peasant revolt in England, which saw alliances of peasants with minor gentry and clerical leaders claiming to act on behalf of the commons, or the commonwealth. Governments found that language not just commented on but played back to them in highly critical terms.[17] There was a fateful tension here, though, in expressing loyalty to the supposed order of the commonwealth while posing such an open challenge to it in practice. Governments at the time, and historians since then, have been much more impressed by the radicalism of the challenge than by the claim to political respectability, and with good reason. Certainly, the life expectancy of a leader of a peasant revolt was short, and the direct effect of rebellion usually government repression. But the possibility of revolt exercised a restraint on government. Speaking to the English parliament in the hard decade of the 1590s, Fulke Greville, for example, worried that 'If the feet knew their strength as we know their oppression, they would not bear as they do.'[18]

By then peasant revolt was dying out. This was partly because the peasantry was disappearing—English villages were increasingly divided between a prosperous middling sort aligned with the comforts and values of gentry life, and a poorer sort of tenants and wage labourers set apart by their poverty. Village leaders were more likely to identify with the existing social order than a potentially subversive view of the commonwealth. At the same time the vision of society as a commonwealth was giving way in public discussion to a language of orders. On this view the social order was made up of different sorts of people with distinct functions—it was not (as we might think nowadays) an agglomeration of individuals who are fundamentally equal, but rather a coordinated social body consisting of different parts, each of which had to perform a distinct purpose if the whole body was to work healthily. As Greville might have put it, the feet were there to bear the rest of the body, not to do the work of the brain.[19]

A new possibility was signalled during the English revolution, though, clearly represented in a famous image of the execution of

Figure 14. The execution of the earl of Strafford, 1641

the earl of Strafford in 1641 by Wenceslas Hollar. In it, the earl and his executioner are barely visible—the subject is really the huge crowd of people, unnaturally calm apart from the man in the foreground struggling to climb a platform to get a view. Hollar seems to want us to focus on the large crowd that witnessed this killing (Figure 14).

This seems to depict a new collectivity, a successor to the peasant army. The crowd is made up of individuals gathered as witnesses to public life. The term 'the people' took off during the 1640s, as partisans appealed to the public for support for their version of the war, or the peace. The chaotic course of the war, and the equally chaotic public discussion about it, created uncertainty about what was happening, what it meant, and who should decide such argument. In such circumstances the arbitration of the people was seen as one way out and, although not everyone was drawn to it initially, it had a long afterlife.

Moments of rebellion, or direct action in the name of the commonwealth or the people, mobilize collective *force* independently of government. Historians often celebrate them as moments of the liberation of those excluded from formal power, but of course they are not always directed to good political ends, and they sometimes hurt the innocent. A group exercising what it sees as legitimate force can end up doing terrible things. Catholic priests were lynched in the 1640s, ethnic minorities terrorized in race riots in the nineteenth and twentieth centuries, and religious sectarian hostilities retain their malevolent potential in areas of the United Kingdom. Direct appeal to the people undercuts the institutional restraints and conventions that maintain political order and decency. People who believe in popular sovereignty are not necessarily comfortable with populism, therefore.

This is because an obvious advantage of institutionalized politics is constraint. Institutions can be corrupt and are capable of even more appalling things but there are means, however notional, of holding them to account—that is the essence of institutionalization, after all. Collective mobilization has no such restraint. However virtuous and necessary the cause, the threat is that once in train there are no controls over collective action, no effective way to hold participants to account for unjust actions. The great virtue of institutionalizing power is to restrain and channel political passions; the great cost is that doing so locks some groups into power and others out. The corruption of institutions invites attempts at reform or revolution, but risks setting free unrestrained political passions. Populism is one way to challenge institutionalized corruption, inertia, or ineffectiveness—to 'drain the swamp' or 'burst the Westminster bubble'—but the costs of unleashing political passions can be enormous. Perhaps the cardinal demonstration of this from the British past is the crisis of the mid-seventeenth century: those conditions gave unprecedented power to people outside government and allowed the expression of radical views; but it was also a deeply traumatic experience.

Collective power is in itself morally neutral—whether exercised through institutions, or mobilized outside them, it can be used to good or bad ends. Collective power outside institutions, like that exercised through institutions, is shaped by ideas, material conditions, and the broader institutional landscape. It can recall a collective institution to its agreed purposes and drive reform; it can also, like the corruption of collective institutions, be a force for evil ends. The struggle, as with institutional politics, is to make a reality of claims to legitimacy.

Informal Spaces, Alternate Worlds, Making a Life

Just as people have imagined alternate worlds, so they actually created them: spaces where people can live by alternative rules or escape the oppression of dominant values. Sixteenth-century alehouses have been seen as offering this kind of space for the poor to enjoy fellowship and sociability on their terms rather than those set by their social superiors—a world quite apart from the fancier inns and taverns. It caused governments to worry that these spaces were really alternate worlds from which dangerously subversive politics might spring. The same was true of separatist congregations and informal forms of religious fellowship. In eighteenth-century London Mother Clap's Molly House hosted same-sex encounters and cross-dressing—a refuge, in a way, for individuals whose lives, identity, or choices were not acceptable to wider society. In that sense this is a form of agency, achieved by withdrawal, creating an alternative world in defined spaces for limited periods of time.

The Mangrove Café in London offered a similar space for Black Britons in the 1960s. From such spaces, though, spring other possibilities—opportunities for stronger self-assertion and an example or inspiration to others. The Mangrove, for example, was raided by the police twelve times between January 1969 and July 1970. That harassment became the launchpad for an inspiring assertion of Black rights, based on some powerful appropriations. After the last of these raids 150 people demonstrated at the local police station in protest, and nine of them were arrested for riot and affray. In the course of a fifty-five-day trial at the Old Bailey they argued, among other things, that only a Black jury could hear them fairly—an extension of the right to be heard by one's peers, enshrined in Magna Carta and championed by many others since. Five of the defendants were acquitted of all charges and the other four were acquitted of the most serious charge of riot. Most fundamentally, they appropriated the official claim that we are all equal before the law to challenge racism. The judge acknowledged that the trial had 'regrettably shown evidence of racial hatred on both sides': official recognition that racism had shaped police action, that in practice everyone was not equal in the eyes of the law (Figure 15).[20]

There is a broader point here, about the ways individuals can create a little space for themselves by taking advantage of the world they encounter simply to try to make a life. The Roman empire offered opportunities not only to topple or change tribal leaders, but to make a life. For example, the Londinium building boom of the first century offered employment to Boduacus—a

Figure 15. The Mangrove Café

name suggestive of Gaulish origins—as well as to the more Roman-sounding Titus (or Potitus). In western Kent at the same time Cabriabanus built a decent business as a tiler—his distinctive stamp appears on many surviving tiles. Other tilers complained that one of their number, Augustalis, wandered off from work each day. One curse tablet at Bath is in an undecipherable language, perhaps one native to Britain and otherwise unknown but nonetheless taking advantage of Roman baths and Gods. Many of the 200 names recorded in the Vindolanda tablets are from the Rhine, revealing how the empire created an opportunity for people who were not born Roman, even if they may have come to see themselves that way. In fact, a tomb for Regina near the Wall at South Shields reveals such a story in some detail. Originally a Catuvellauni from Hertfordshire, she had been enslaved but then freed, and married Barates, a man from Palmyra in Syria.

His tombstone reveals that he was a trader in ensigns (military symbols or standards)—two people making their lives within the embrace of the empire.[21]

Space can be made in apparently unpromising conditions. In 1066 an Anglo-Saxon woman called Aelfgyth held half a hide of land in Oakley, Buckinghamshire. She was a 'maid' (that is, unmarried) and so we might think relatively vulnerable in that society, but she enjoyed the land at the gift of the Sheriff, Godric, in return for teaching his daughter how to do gold embroidery. We do not know anything about what she thought, but the glimpse we have of her in Domesday book reveals her using a skill that was in demand to offset the disadvantages that went along with being female in the eleventh century.[22]

The growth of Atlantic trade and empire created such opportunities, even for some Africans. As Europeans became aware of the rest of the world in the sixteenth and seventeenth centuries, Africans returned to Britain, perhaps for the first time since the Romans, making their lives on the island through the expansion of European trade. John Blanke arrived in 1501, possibly as part of the entourage of Catherine of Aragon: an African at a Spanish court. He was able to make a life at the English court as a skilled trumpeter, present at the funeral of Henry VII in 1509 and at the celebrations of the birth of his grandson Henry in 1511. Blanke petitioned for more money and got married—European expansion into the Atlantic had given him an opportunity to make his way in a world that we would have imagined closed to him. Sixty years later Francis Drake had four Africans with him on his circumnavigation of the globe, 'Cimaroons' who had come on board on an earlier expedition to Panama, helping him to raid Spanish shipping, and who had chosen to return to England with him.[23]

When English settlers arrived in Jamestown, Virginia in 1608 they had with them some young boys, including Thomas Savage, about whom we know nothing really. He was given to Wahunseneca (Powhatan), who ruled most of the tribes in the area, and met Pocahontas. The theory was that adolescents like Thomas were wet clay that could be easily moulded by their environment, in this case by learning the language and culture of the native inhabitants more easily than the adults could. In addition to being a pawn in a diplomatic game, therefore, Thomas (along with other young boys) could become a cultural mediator. In this way a boy of very obscure origins achieved influence, mediating between cultures, and securing a place among the advisers to both communities. It was a complicated existence that bred distrust as well as respect in both communities, but it was a kind of agency made possible by the new conditions of Atlantic trade.[24]

In the following century Captain Cook's ship was full of men taking opportunities—not least Sir Joseph Banks, Daniel Solander, and Sydney Parkinson who all took a big step up in the world through their role in the expedition. The voyage depended, though, on the advice of a Polynesian, Tupaia, who chose to join the ship at Ra'iatea, and who guided it through the Pacific islands. He was an educated man who commanded respect wherever they went, and had apparently joined the voyage in order to learn more of the English. In fact William Anderson, the ship's surgeon, had joined the voyage to 'see a people following the dictates of nature without being bias'd by education' but came to realize that he was as much the object of enquiry as the inquirer.[25] Nelson had a number of crewmen of African origin with him in the early nineteenth century, one of them immortalized at the foot of Nelson's column.[26] Just as the expansion of the Roman empire created opportunities for ordinary people to make new lives, and discover new things, so too did the European expansion into the Atlantic and Pacific.

The British empire continued do this into the twentieth century. For example, academically gifted West Indians of C. L. R. James's generation were treated to a version of a British public school education. James's own erudition and literary skill opened a world of opportunity for him which was expressed, ultimately, in the campaign for West Indian independence and the Pan-African movement. The experience he had when he encountered the reality of British life was productively at odds with the expectation he had as a result of his pro-British education in Trinidad. A key element of this was cricket. Himself a fine cricketer, he accompanied Learie Constantine to Lancashire in the 1930s, seeing at first-hand how Constantine's skills as a cricketer allowed him to carve out a life there. On James's account Constantine was non-confrontational, but his dignity and manners also made a point about his value as an individual. His example was empowering for others, and educational for those white Britons who were willing to learn.[27]

Political change helps shape the context in which ordinary lives are made and offers shifting opportunities even for those who do not try to exert direct political agency. Simply trying to make a dignified life can become the basis for critical political action, as it did at the Mangrove Café, but it can also be an end in itself.

Historicizing Agency: Representation, Deliberation, Administration

During the twentieth century a welfare state took shape that aimed to provide material security, health care, and education to the population. That was undoubtedly a response to the growth of mass politics and the ballot box: the organized appeal to voters by established parties. It was also associated at times with policies of economic redistribution, using the tax system to move wealth from the rich to the poor. We might also point to the success of the Suffragettes, and indeed the earlier movements of franchise reform that had given greater influence to men excluded from formal participation in politics. The longer battle to give greater freedoms to women—free contraception, support for childcare arrangements to allow a return to work, or for equal pay—has parallels in the success of other groups in securing improvements to their social position. There have been successes too in legislation to protect ethnic and religious minorities from hate crimes and discrimination, or repealing the laws against homosexuality, for example.

Much of this is a reflection of the power of the electorate. It would be hard to argue that ordinary people had the same power to affect legislation before parliament acquired executive power and answered directly to the electorate. This has been a great gain. However, over time ordinary people have lost other kinds of agency. Firstly, it seems that access to the law has been in decline since the seventeenth century, and that should give us pause for thought. Secondly, the proceedings of parliament in earlier periods were much more open—during the seventeenth and eighteenth centuries parliament was a porous institution, with members of the public freely gathering in the precincts and at the door of the House of Commons and of its committee meetings.[28] Party organization and the power of party whips mean that MPs are often simply lobby fodder, but when they do break ranks and vote with their consciences, they can be denounced as betraying their mandate. In that situation they are seen as members of a party elected to govern rather than representatives elected to deliberate on the process of law-making.

Perhaps even more importantly, the adoption of universal voting has been accompanied by the development of formal bureaucracy. As we saw in the previous chapter, between 900 and 1300 local assemblies played a critical role in English governance, operated quite autonomously, and consisting in theory of all free men.[29] In the sixteenth and seventeenth centuries the local experience of authority was usually an encounter with a local notable, holding an office. There were ways in which they were susceptible to pressure—they could be embarrassed or shamed into action, or into not taking action that was formally required but locally unhelpful. Of course, that was a system wid open to pressure from particular interest groups, and gave local notables enormous personal power, but it was also a more responsive system than modern bureaucracy.

Nineteenth-century reform swept this system away. It was driven to a significant degree by a desire to tame the urban environment and improve public health, producing a centralizing set of reforms: a new poor law, municipal corporations, public health boards. Local officeholders were replaced by professional state employees: constables becoming policemen, regulation of public institutions put in the hands of inspectors of factories, schools, and prisons. It was mainly an urban phenomenon, resulting in many new institutions and rural governance atrophied—Quarter Sessions the parish, the hundred, the improvement commissions. The participatory culture of local governance had gone.[30] The formal position now is that electorates influence parliament, and that bureaucracies implement the resulting measures uniformly and universally. Discretion in this system is a dirty word, akin to corruption.

That something has been lost is demonstrated by the modern hostility to 'faceless bureaucrats' and 'jobsworths'. It was this problem of bureaucratic accountability that John Major's government sought to address in the 'citizens' charter' initiative—that administrative bodies would enter into contracts with ordinary citizens and be answerable for their conduct. Much derided initially, this has now been taken up very widely, suggesting that it does fill some kind of gap in collective agency.[31] Above all, of course, hostility to unaccountable bureaucracy has lighted on the EU—often said to be composed entirely of such people, and unlike their UK counterparts, not restrained by an electorate.

*   *   *

It is hard to talk about agency without talking about its limits, and for any period of history we can point to groups of people not empowered by political life in any real sense, for any length of time. Throughout the period covered in the book there were individuals and groups who were in effect on Britain but not in Britain: resident here, but not fully included in the political communities on the island. The history of these exclusions is not a marginal issue, but a way of understanding central features of those political communities. What David Olusoga has said about Black history—that it is actually central to the experience and imagination of the whole political community[32]—is also true of other forms of identity—class, sexuality, religion, gender.

This is no simple story of progress, then. Political influence has been won and lost continuously, not distributed once and for all in a single battle. This tempers the otherwise justified optimism about the power of the ballot box. The direct mandate from the ballot box is of course important, but perhaps less so than the *idea* of representation—the claim that politicians are representing the people—which offers an important hostage to fortune. Despite all these reservations, however, democratic institutions can be highly responsive. We live in a very unequal society, of course: extreme inequalities of wealth are associated with catastrophic effects on life chances for those most excluded. However, other forms of exclusion, exploitation, and suffering have been overcome in the past; the burden of proof is on those who think that the ones we currently face cannot be.

7

CHANGE OVER TIME

Phases in the History of Political Life

Bitish history is usually divided up according to changes in the dominant power on the island. Thus, although the Romans never governed the whole island, we talk about Roman Britain, and much of the rest of the story is divided according to which dynasties were in control in England—for example, at 1066 (the Norman conquest of England but not Scotland or Wales) and 1485 (the accession of the Tudors in England and Wales but not in Scotland). Even this division of the British past is inconsistent, however. For the periods prior to the arrival of the Romans we talk about the past in terms of phases in human technologies (the Ages of Stone and Bronze for example), while historians relate British history in the twentieth century to the politics of the world at large—the inter-war, Cold War, or post-9/11 periods, for example.

Clearly the past can be divided in many different ways, and it is difficult to apply a consistent principle. Even in this brief book we can see how phases in the history of ideas, material life, and organizational capacity can be complex and overlapping. This chapter offers an overview of the continuous interaction of these factors in shaping the political life of people on the island. It does so in relation to:

- the impact of broader material and technological changes: for example, the development of farming, continuous environmental change, the development of long-distance trade within and beyond Europe, or the growth of the carbon economy;
- the impact of ideas: the shift associated, for example, with the arrival of the Beaker people, the impact of Roman ideas of government, the Christian conversions, the development of dynastic and feudal politics, the impact of renaissance, reformation, and enlightenment, and the mark made by rival views of the capitalist economy (liberal, socialist, communist, and neoliberal) and of transnational ideals such as peace, environmental, and human rights movements;
- the effects of changing organizational capacity: for example, the encounter with Rome and the Vikings, the growth of dynastic kingdoms and maritime empires, the development of nation states, and the post-war growth of transnational and supranational organizations.

It is a fluid history, driven by the interplay of collective and differential power and the shifting relationships between the scales of collective organization. Change is also driven by the kinds of problems that were being addressed and the ideas that were used to define them and shape responses. This is a continuous process and any division is artificial, but it gives us a framework in which to understand any particular moment.

The Neolithic to the Iron Age: Material History, Identity, and Collective Power

The earliest human tools so far discovered on Great Britain may be over 900,000 years old. Since that time, what is now Britain seems to have been abandoned by humans at least seven times, as the climate deteriorated: human occupation moved to the rhythm of the climate. These varying species of human hunter-gatherer can be distinguished by the tools they made, but they left few traces of their lives on the landscape. The surviving cave art at Cresswell Crags on the Derbyshire/Nottinghamshire border gives a tantalizing glimpse of the internal life of some hunters at what was perhaps a summer camp during the last ice age. Despite its great age, it is separated from the finds at Happisburgh and Pakefield on the East Anglian coast by hundreds of thousands of years: it was the product in fact of a different human species. There are no buildings or other major marks on the landscape to reveal the collective life of any of these groups from across this vast expanse of time, although the evidence from modern hunter-gatherers is that collective and cooperative action is essential to their lives.

For our purposes, therefore, the most dramatic change in collective life on Britain came between 4,200 and 3,800 years ago, with the rapid adoption of farming. Following that transition we have a much clearer view of the uses of collective power and increasingly revealing glimpses of the ideas that mobilized them. The new food-producing strategy arrived at the same time as new gene lines and may have been the product of migration. In any case, it is quickly associated with durable changes to the landscape—initially the construction of long barrows, mortuary enclosures, cursus monuments, and deep flint mines. These are the first material evidence of the uses of collective power and, as we have seen, at the large henge and stone circle monuments that followed within 1,500 years, we have a sense of some of the ideas that shaped this collective life. Thereafter it is possible to trace some relatively rapid changes in collective activity and ideas— notably, for example, in the arrival of the Beaker people, which signalled the end of megalith building and the related ritual land- scapes. Instead, the visible changes in the landscape tended to be the construction of barrows that marked the lives of individuals or smaller groups, perhaps family lineages. They take their name from the fine ceramic beakers associated with their sites, which also reveal copper-working and in some places fortified settle- ments: they were new arrivals, as modern DNA research has dem- onstrated, and brought with them new technologies but also new beliefs reflected in their collective action.

These Neolithic and Bronze Age societies engaged in long- distance trade—Jadeite axes from around 5,000 or 6,000 years ago link sites that are 1,500km apart. Stonehenge, as we have seen, seems to have been a focal point for people from across the whole of Great Britain, and the Beaker people exchanged metal, jet, and amber over long distances. Human settlement in this part of Europe was shaped by climate, exchange, and migration, and at each stage represented a history both connected to these wider movements and parallel to responses elsewhere. Henges, for example, seem to have been distinctive to Britain, although in technological, aesthetic, and perhaps world view they share some- thing with collective life elsewhere. On the other hand, at various points it is possible to see regional distinctions in material culture and building styles across Britain, associated too with different trading worlds—along the Atlantic coast, from southern Britain to northern France, or along the Rhine corridor, for example.

In the 1,500 years before the Romans arrived there is more evidence of the internal organization of these societies—division of the land, the survival of homesteads, and hilltop forts—evidence probably of a more socially stratified warrior society, based around fighting and feasting, a development which was common across Europe. About 800 BCE, with the arrival of iron, the archaeological record reveals a society of fortifications and strongly defended homesteads, in which chariots and horses were prized possessions and included in burials. Agriculture seems to have intensified, and the land was divided. Trade brought southern Britain into the orbit of the advancing Roman empire, and there is evidence of military cooperation between tribes on two sides of the channel. As Roman attention turned to Great Britain, we get the first evidence of internal politics—the names of leaders and political groups, and evidence of political dispute.

For most of this period, though, from the first human presence to the arrival of the Romans, we can see the effect of material change much more easily than institutional or ideological innovation—the effects of environment (in the ebb and flow of the human presence), economic change (such as the adoption of farming), and technological change (stone, bronze, and iron, for example) rather than the spread of a new understanding of how society should be ordered, the arrival of the Beaker people being a partial but important exception. We can trace all this as part of both a shared and parallel history, which played out differently on different parts of the island.

Although this is a rich picture, then, it lacks a detailed political dimension. The evidence is just not very revealing about power relations. The agency we can see is primarily collective—the power to construct on the scale of Stonehenge or Silbury Hill. We cannot say much about the power of one group over another, or how that was sustained, challenged, or changed over time: we do not know much about their collective institutions, in other words. We know hardly anything about the interior lives of these people, their collective goals or beliefs, or about the patterns of political agency available to them. Although the effects of these things are plain in the landscape and there is a rich literature on the cognitive capacities that underlay that kind of collective action, much about the life of these complex societies is now hidden from us.

55 BCE to 950: The Impact of Rome, Christianity, and the Vikings

Rome was both a highly organized and a literate society, and the extension of Roman authority onto a large part of Great Britain throws much more light on these issues. The archaeological record speaks volumes for the organizational capacity of the Romans—the road system, the foundation of towns, the building of spectacular villas, and, of course, Hadrian's Wall. Where previous transformations visible in the archaeology seem to have had material origins, the Roman invasion was obviously driven by institutional and ideological dynamics—the need for great men to achieve military glory and spoils in support of their political ambitions. Nonetheless, the arrival of the Romans had profound material and economic effects.

The geography of the impact is varied, though. In the south and east of Britain roads, towns, and villas give evidence of a province fully integrated into the empire, its material culture a product of long-distance trade and its products supplying the empire. Further north and west, however, the impact of Rome in the archaeology is less marked. There is less evidence of villa society, and the remains are more clearly those of a militarized region. Beyond Hadrian's Wall and to the west, in Wales and Cornwall, Roman remains become quite sparse. These regions were undoubtedly engaged with Rome—diplomatically and economically, and not just as hostile neighbours—but judging from the archaeological record, the encounter worked in a different way. Roman goods are less abundant, and the presence of Rome may have led to the consolidation of independent territories around it, partly as elites were able to control the flow of Roman goods.

In the most Romanized zone we have some access to ideas and agency, although less than we might imagine. What was going on in Roman Britain is often known from external sources, and interpolation—filling in the gaps in the evidence on the basis of knowledge about how Romanized society operated elsewhere. Nonetheless, we can see the impact of Roman ideas of civility and get glimpses of how ordinary people shaped or took advantage of the uses of political power. Outside that zone we know little: reports at second-hand of the names and locations of 'tribes' and their relations with each other and the Romans, but this reveals very little of their collective lives.

If the impact of Rome varied geographically, it was also in some ways shallow. By 500, villas and towns had disappeared from the south and east, along with many of the skills that had flourished within the Roman orbit—building in masonry, for example. The collapse of Roman institutions was more complete on Great Britain than elsewhere in Europe as the former province splintered into a series of kingdoms. These seem to have been warrior kingdoms, initially based around kinship, fighting, protection, and personal loyalty and probably less clearly defined by territory, although by 550 succession to leadership was probably by inheritance. Unlike the Roman system, they depended on lordship not taxation— personal loyalties and service rather than public institutions and citizenship—and they were much smaller than Roman provinces. In this respect the differences between parts of the island had probably narrowed. The territory of modern Scotland had four kingdoms, assumed to be largely of this kind, although there is slender evidence from this period that might suggest the existence of tax- raising powers as well as hereditary authority.

Over the long run the arrival of Christianity was probably more transformative than the direct influence of the Romans. The impact was reflected in what kings claimed they would and should do, and on the demands their subjects could make of them. In the south and east it was Roman rather than Celtic Christianity, and that brought back with it elements of Roman ideals and imagery. Over the centuries after the end of Roman authority it seems that societies had become more differentiated, with larger gaps between elite and ordinary lives. At the same time, authority, as well as being inherited, was attached to a stable territory: warrior tribes were being supplanted by dynastic kingdoms, and Christian values worked to support the position of kings. This may also have increased the gap between parts of the island, as these developments proceeded more slowly in some places than others.

Christianity was a key element of this new form of kingship, but not straightforwardly the cause or template. Institutional development was associated with these new ideas but was also underpinned by economic recovery following post-Roman collapse.

Nonetheless, Christianity was of critical importance, and delivered new kinds of agency—it provided values against which political claims could be made which were not simply controlled by kings, and increasingly there was an alternative source of institutional power too. Most obviously, Christian values and practice created opportunities for (a small number of aristocratic) women and the Church was potentially at least an alternative source of authority and protection. Christianity and the Church offered opportunities for appropriation and triangulation, in other words: agency may not have been new, but some of the ways it could be possible are clearer.

These Christian, territorial, dynastic structures were a distinctive form of political organization, akin to those on the continent—Charlemagne, King of the Franks and then Emperor of the Carolingian empire (768–814), seems often to have been a direct model to be emulated. This was a parallel history, then, but also a shared one in the influence of Charlemagne and the influence of Roman Christianity; Roman political values may often have been re-imported from these sources rather than survivals of the Roman presence. It was less true of the Scottish and Pictish kingdoms, as far as we can tell, which were more connected to Irish forms.

Viking expansion, the third key influence during this period, impinged on varying political forms, therefore. In the south and east of the island it helped to accelerate the consolidation of an English kingdom with coordinated military and taxing powers and developed legal codes. These Anglo-Saxon arrangements were subsequently assumed to be a critical part of the political inheritance of the whole island. It is certainly a commonsensical set of arrangements to modern eyes—dynastic succession to an English throne, with burghs, churches, and a common law. As an account of life on Great Britain in the Anglo-Saxon period, however, it ignores the Danelaw and the succession of Danish kings to the English throne. Moreover, in the area of modern Scotland and Wales the Viking influence was less dramatic—taking the form mainly of agricultural settlements with trading connections to the North, primarily Norway, via the Irish Sea coasts.

By 950 these influences—Rome, Christianity, and the Vikings—had produced dynastic kingdoms defined by territory rather than kinship on the south of the island, with similar although perhaps more restricted developments in the north. They were parallel and connected to developments elsewhere, notably in the Carolingian Kingdom, and these forces for change were of course operating over much larger territories. Rome's empire extended from the Middle East, through the Mediterranean and much of North and Western Europe. Christendom was larger still, while the Viking diaspora stretched from the Black Sea to the coasts of North America.

It is possible to say quite a lot about the exercise of political power and its restraint in some parts of the island at that time. Perhaps the most dramatic example of the dialogue between collective and differential power is the Danegeld—the mobilization of private wealth for a public purpose on a huge scale which led to a significant transfer of money to Scandinavia. The way it was paid provided a model and precedent for centuries—an example of the broader path dependency arising from the particular local response to the wider pressures of the Roman and post-Roman period.

Dynastic Kingdoms I: 950–1300

There is a broad pattern in politics from around 950 to around 1650—dynastic kingdoms defined territorially, with stable rules of inheritance, governed alongside the Church. Inheritance was frequently unstable in practice, and relations with the Church not always harmonious. Dynasts secured their interests through war and marriage, a pattern common across the whole of Eurasia. At times warfare imposed heavy burdens and pushed monarchs to enter increasingly explicit and formal contracts with their subjects—offering, for example, protection, justice, and powers of self-government in return for service, money, and loyalty. Kingdoms were de-stabilized by discontents framed in these ways—claims about the conduct of the monarch in relation to these deals, by the succession and by relations with the Church, all of which offered ways to challenge or restrain kings. Political life was also affected by intellectual movements in Christianity and the Church, and the complexion of royal authority shifted as ideas about law, honour, and virtue changed. Agency was exercised by appropriating those languages, rights, and privileges, or by applying pressure to these institutions.

It is convenient (though of course artificial) to divide this broad period of government around 1300. By that point the proliferation of formal institutions had created a complex political society which in the following centuries operated under the pressures of expensive and extensive warfare, some dramatic economic shocks, and religious dispute.[1]

The Norman conquest had led to the wholesale imposition of feudal relations in the Kingdom of England and by the thirteenth century royal power was institutionalized and regulated through powers of taxation and representation, the increasing formalization of the role of parliament, the codification of the common law which shaped royal justice, and the creation of boroughs. Again, these developments were common across the island, although they did not develop in the Scottish kingdom at the same rate. The consolidation of a Kingdom of Scotland along these lines is traditionally associated with Kenneth Mac Alpin in the tenth century, although the subsequent influence of feudal relations was more piecemeal and the development of royal authority thereafter more tempered by local rights and lordship. The Welsh principality forged by Llywelyn the Great in the thirteenth century was fundamentally shaped by the institutional model of the Kingdom of England, and partly by its direct intervention.

A structural feature of these hereditary monarchies was disputed succession, an opportunity for disaffected nobles in particular to challenge royal authority. In England there was repeated instability produced by rival claims to the throne, starting in the short reign of King Harold II (1066), while unstable succession in Scotland was, for example, an opportunity for English aggression under Edward I.

These kingdoms were dynastic rather than national institutions, their geography following family interests rather than national lines: in the case of the Kingdom of England, for example, to extensive interests in France. The politics of Christendom were a further connection beyond the island—in the battles between the developing institutions of royal and papal authority, of which the dispute with Thomas Becket was a local example, or the participation in the Crusades.

Although there was economic, material, and technological change, with the exception of the costs of war, it is hard to see it as driving political life in the period before 1300. The costs of war, like the middle class, are always rising, but during the thirteenth century they clearly drove innovation in the relationship between monarchs and their subjects, facilitating ambitious military spending, of which Conwy Castle is perhaps a clear example. An increasingly elaborate institutional landscape was associated with the development of new ideas, though—in particular the idea of the public good served and protected by the king, which was distinct from the web of particular rights and duties owed one to another by lords, tenants, boroughs, and abbots. These institutions and ideas were also a source of agency. Boroughs, for example, were given local control of markets and their courts were a means to tackle local problems and a platform for the expression of local interests to the monarch. These local institutions fostered and expressed local identities too. Finally, they created an institutional culture which provided the tools to contest royal power, manifest, for example, in the troubles of King John's reign leading to the signing of Magna Carta. This became a regular pattern of behaviour as influential subjects—Simon de Montfort and his successors—sought institutional restraints on royal power, and it was a feature of European politics more broadly.

Alongside this developing royal authority was an increasingly elaborate and powerful ecclesiastical structure. This too was a source of opportunity and potential agency: the triangulation of authority. In a sense this was at the heart of the Becket dispute, which focused on the treatment of 'criminous clerks', and the potential for a subject of the king to opt to be tried by a different authority. But there was a more general potential that the Church might provide an alternative set of values, and movements of reform in the Church had implications for political authority, even if this potential was not much realized before the fourteenth century.

Anglo-Saxon law depended on the activity of local assemblies consisting of all freemen, but in general the agency of ordinary people is not easily visible for much of this period and there were certainly very significant formal exclusions. Serfdom, for example, excluded people from access to royal justice and imposed tight restrictions on their personal and economic freedoms. Nonetheless, by the end of the thirteenth century there was a dense network of formal liberties and jurisdictions, and jurisdictional rivalries that may have offered some people the opportunities for triangulation that the politics of the royal succession or of Christendom did for the great nobility. Representative institutions worked for a narrow elite, though, and it is not clear how much pressure they felt or acknowledged from others. Lords promised protection and justice, but it is hard to know what reality that had, or how easy it was to hold them to account by those values.

Dynastic Kingdoms II: 1300–1650

During the fourteenth century catastrophic population loss in England coincided with an extended period of continental warfare. By 1300 a population high had been reached. The subsequent collapse in the face of famine and plague dramatically changed the bargaining positions of various groups in English society, at a time when the Crown was making increased demands to support its wars. While the influence of dynastic politics remained critical at the top of the kingdom, there were profound changes in the relationships between kings, lords, and subjects: those who survived the Black Death were in a stronger position to negotiate with lords, and the need for taxation required successive monarchs to negotiate with parliaments, major boroughs, and their aristocracy. Thereafter, the active engagement of ordinary people with collective institutions is increasingly visible. The Scottish kingdom developed in a similar direction, but not under such pressure.

Political life was also shaped by three other dynamics: the further development of local government and popular politics; the impact of international intellectual movements—the renaissance and reformation; and the changing technology of war.

During these centuries the institutions of royal government continued to develop, particularly in the English kingdom—the common law and the system of courts, parliaments, and boroughs. Manor courts continued to regulate important aspects of local life—the management of the land and other resources, environmental measures, social and moral control, and minor interpersonal disputes. The Church, through its courts, the ministrations of the parish, and the local role of religious houses, could also loom large in the economic, social, and moral regulation of local life. Increasingly it relied on 'trustworthy men': local inhabitants of relatively humble status who could be relied upon to report to the Church and act on its directions. They exercised, through the Church, considerable influence over local life.[2]

Between the Peasants' Revolt in 1381 and Kett's rebellion in 1549 there were periodic peasant revolts in England. We might think of this form of politics ultimately as a demand for recognition rather than an effective intervention, since it so often ended in repression. It was partly, though, a product of formal politics, drawing on the idea of the common good that was used to legitimate the role of the Crown. This was true of less spectacular forms of political action too—small-scale riots, and other forms of pressure on governors to use their power to serve the public good. The organizational capacity which allowed more effective responses to plague and dearth also created opportunities for ordinary people to call government to account, or to deploy its power for their own purposes. There was a litigation boom in sixteenth- and seventeenth-century England, so that this was perhaps the period in which it was least true to say that law provided rich men with justice. The Kingdom of Scotland remained institutionally distinct, and is less well documented, but the evidence points to similar developments—the elaboration of royal government and of the authority of the Scottish parliament.

Renaissance ideas played an important part in this, placing renewed emphasis on the common good and the role of the commonwealth in promoting it; but so too did the European reformation, which sometimes generated pressure to achieve not just personal redemption but social reform. Measures taken to deal with poverty reflect all these influences—renaissance and reformation, and institutional development.[3] However, it was the urban and middling sort who gained most from these measures of regulation and discipline, and those below them in the social order who felt its bite.

Changes in political communication were critical in allowing the formation of new collective interests. This too was related to institutional development—during the sixteenth and seventeenth centuries, for example, the increasingly important role of parliaments fuelled the development of petitioning; borough charters were not just a source of political education for the town in question, but invited discussion and observation of other chartered powers in something like an urban system. These institutions disseminated government language, providing the resource with which those outside government could make counter-claims. Print accelerated this—a key tool for institution-building and official communication, but also a way for people to make common cause outside government.

Another major technological influence was the development of gunpowder weapons. From the early sixteenth century onwards, European governments made increasing use of them, making war more expensive: the weapons themselves were costly and making effective use of them required more elaborate drill and training. There were similar developments at sea, as specialized fighting ships developed. The English kingdom was not engaged in large-scale European warfare for most of the sixteenth century and made only halting adjustments to the new demands of warfare, and the Scottish kingdom was even more insulated. Nonetheless, there was pressure to increase government revenues, and this produced political tensions of various kinds in England from the mid-sixteenth century and in Scotland in the early seventeenth.

Catastrophic losses in France changed the geography of ambition for kings in England. Wales was fully absorbed into this political system in 1536—given local government structures akin to those in England and representation in the Westminster parliament. In the 1540s the English Crown created a Kingdom of Ireland, hoping thereby to make a reality of the Lordship claimed in Ireland since the twelfth century. The Union of the Crowns in 1603 meant that for the first time Great Britain was under a single monarch, although not in a single monarchy, and its fate was linked to a third monarchy across the Irish Sea.

The reformation had different effects in each of the Three Kingdoms, so that they each felt the pressures of religious and governmental reform in different ways, while the inhabitants of each watched events in the other two in order to try to understand their monarch's real intentions. This was important context for the mid-seventeenth-century crisis, which was to fundamentally shape relationships within the UK and between Britons and the Irish over the next 400 years. It also fed the development of fiscal-military institutions under parliamentary control within the shell of a dynastic kingdom: a hybrid of a dynastic kingdom and an emerging national state.

A Hybrid State with a Maritime Empire: 1650–1800

As a result of this crisis, England had the military and financial capacity to enter maritime trade on equal terms with the leading European states. Over the next 150 years the union with Scotland and then Ireland became the basis for a British empire, built around trade and naval power, and increasingly reinforced by the British manufacturing industry. Dynastic politics continued to be important, and major challenges to the regime in 1685, 1688, 1715, and 1745 were led by alternate claimants to the throne, and that in 1688 proved successful. But this was increasingly a parliamentary not a monarchical state—financial and executive authority migrated into parliament, and ideas of representation and national interest played a more prominent role in public debate. During the eighteenth century the leading figures in parliament began to be referred to as prime ministers—their political position depended on their command of parliament, not court.

Another important legacy of the English revolution was political partisanship in popular politics. The English civil war had mobilized a huge proportion of the male population, claimed a very large number of lives, destroyed property, and made fortunes. Parliament's increasingly important political role made it the focus for lobbying on a more and more concerted scale. A growing urban society, informed by a lively print industry, was becoming engaged in national politics through parliament: the collective power coordinated under the Crown had increased dramatically, and called forth new forms of restraint, or attempted restraint. Through print people who would never have met in real life were able to inform one another of what was going on, and form solidarities (or hostilities) over great distances. This created new communities of shared belief, and they kept a close eye on the detail of national politics and the actions of politicians. These were new sources of collective agency and a new forum through which to exercise collective restraint on the powerful.

A further legacy of the seventeenth century was religious diversity, which gave individuals more power to worship with people of a like mind and conscience, and through those communities to achieve the kind of change they wanted to see. This intersected with the growing diversity of urban life and personal consumption, and proliferating possibilities for sexual self-expression. This is a form of agency critical in contemporary life—freedom to express oneself—which is harder to trace in earlier periods (perhaps simply because it is not documented, of course). It is a form of agency—expressive recognition as an individual—visible in earlier periods for elite groups.

Through diverse associational life in towns, the proliferating institutions of government, and the porous and permanent parliament, individuals and groups were able to use these new conditions to get things done. Guilds and civic governments, as well as other lobbying groups, could use private legislation to address local needs, and there was a startling boom in that kind of political action. In the shadow of the American and French revolutions radical groups established corresponding societies, building on this diverse associational life to develop a new vision of the British future too. On the other hand, access to the courts began to close down, perhaps because of a preference for informal arbitration and agreement, although it seems likely that something was lost.

This was true over most of Great Britain. The Welsh gentry and merchants tended to trade in England—east–west routes from north, mid, and south Wales proving easier than those from north to south within Wales. Welsh clubs and societies in London maintained connections between the metropolis and connections at home. Scotland's religion and laws were different, although the Westminster parliament was of critical importance, and we can see there the same social and political developments as those in England. During the eighteenth century, in fact, Scottish intellectuals played a key role in the European enlightenment: notably Adam Smith and David Hume, but others too. In Scotland, however, there was a cultural frontier between this urban, commercial, enlightenment world and the quite different patterns of life in the highlands, and that frontier was overcome by a mixture of military and economic violence.

It was not the only frontier, of course. Up to the 1760s British authority was extending across the North American continent through trade, conquest, and settlement, while in the Caribbean and southern colonies commercial agriculture depended on the enslavement, shipment, and sale of millions of Africans. That pattern of engagement was to be felt across most of the globe during the eighteenth and nineteenth centuries—the loss of the North American colonies did not halt the expansion of British imperial power. As with the Roman empire, there was a carrot as well as a stick, and in the frontier zone those in contact with British authority were tempted to cooperate, not only to resist. The collective institutions of the British empire exercised unprecedented power and could meet the ambitions not just of some Britons but also some of those they colonized. But as with Rome, those institutions also enshrined a marked differential in power, sometimes expressed in atrocity and brutality, and more routinely in the colonization of the mind: the acceptance of the superiority of the life offered by the colonizing power and its values.

The monarchy was receding as a focus of political life, and after 1650 new forms of agency developed, associated with economic growth, urbanization, institutional change, and changing forms of political communication. There were also new opportunities arising from a growing and increasingly interconnected economic world—overseas trade and settlement in particular—but also an increasingly coherent discipline of the poor. However, economic growth also depended to a degree on slavery, a grotesque denial of agency to millions of people.

Industrial Britain, 1800–1945

The growth of empire and trade between 1650 and 1850 was an important economic context for the industrial revolution. Manufacturing growth at home fed a new phase of even more rapid urbanization, and population growth on a hitherto unimagined scale. This rapid urban growth, notably (as ever) of London, but also of new industrial cities in the north and west, created unprecedented social conditions and challenges which demanded new institutional development: as, for example, the major public works which helped overcome the threat of cholera.

Popular politics was also steadily transformed as parliamentary representation broadened and party organizations drove deeper roots. Another critical product of mass politics was the development of Trades Union organization, and of lobbying organizations based on ideological solidarity across a broad social coalition. There is a marked contrast between uncoordinated grain riots which for three centuries had exerted pressure on governments to ensure the supply of food to the poor, and the activities and ambitions of the Anti-Corn Law League in the first half of the nineteenth century. The League, a subscription organization with regular meetings, lobbied for a specific legislative change—the abolition of price supports for food grain which protected domestic farmers—and did so in a formal, targeted, and self-conscious way. This contrast is symptomatic of a broader shift in the mobilization of popular politics. The women's suffrage movement was an heir to this potential, and a reaction to the new possibilities offered by mass participation in parliamentary government. Other forms of identity politics could be promoted this way and official parties also built around them—such as the Primrose League which promoted female engagement with the Tory party in the late nineteenth century. By the end of the first quarter of the twentieth century, formal political participation through the ballot box was a form of agency available to the vast majority of the adult population. However, from the start there were fears about anti-politics: the failure of the people to use or value that form of agency.

Even at the moment of its triumph Westminster was not seen as a natural or the only vehicle through which to express political agency. This was partly because of growing global interdependence, partly a matter of the movement of capital, goods, and people, and partly of the projection of diplomatic and military power. It was also a product of industrial activity. The adoption of mineral-based energy in place of organic energy—the carbon revolution—created shared resource and environmental concerns, and this was later accentuated by the use of electricity. This initially allowed for the portability of power—consumption at very large distances from the place the power was generated—but then later the portability of information and, in recent years, data and trillions of dollars. Industrial society has been an increasingly globally integrated society for all these reasons.

Mass political participation and this new connectivity created the potential for transnational political movements based on particular ideological positions. This was not entirely new. There had been connections between religious reformers across Christendom for centuries. The revolutions in France and America in the late eighteenth century had been understood as addressing connected issues and there were direct connections between some of the revolutionaries. Abolitionism illustrated the potential for political mobilization that was international in its vision and ambition, and other causes were promoted in this way—for example, international communism. It became more visible and more coherent, though, with the development of industry and empire.

Developments in the UK had, during this phase, led and directly shaped developments across the globe. By the late nineteenth century, however, UK manufacturing methods were being adopted and improved upon elsewhere, and other states were contesting British imperial power. These developments posed serious threats to UK imperial hegemony, in the contested scramble for imperial control over Africa or in German armament following the creation of a unitary German state in the later nineteenth century. Mass military mobilization and the application of mechanical methods to combat created the potential for total war—conflict in which the whole society was mobilized. Through two world wars British hegemony was successfully challenged, while a compact was formed in the UK to defend those interests—a 'warfare state' in which science, capital, and government cooperated to defend a national interest. Rising incomes, expanding education, industrial growth, and a continued imperial role were all opportunities, of course, for many ordinary Britons.

Post-War, 1945–2018

The Second World War was fought on an unprecedented geographical scale and intensity. The devastation of entire cities far from the front line revealed the appalling destructive capacity of new technologies, not least in the flattening of Nagasaki and Hiroshima in 1945. War of this kind involved mobilization on a very broad front—scientific, industrial, and economic. Defeat was all the more catastrophic as a result, while victory came at an unprecedented price. Recovery was therefore addressed on a transnational scale: inter-state coordination extended beyond maintaining peace and a balance of power, to the management of the global economy, and expanded thereafter.

The density of this inter-state cooperation—over, for example, nuclear weapons, non-state violence, and more recently the environment—distinguishes the post-war period from what came before. We now confront emerging issues about cyber security and the management of data, and of course the startling pace and scale of capital mobility. Advanced industrial states are more interested than ever in strategic science in the face of these challenges.

Economic behaviour, and by extension economies as a whole, are not ethically or politically neutral. It is inevitable, therefore, that management of the global economy has been a matter of judgement about political economy and a zone of political conflict where competing political economies meet. This produces inter-state tension—over whaling or carbon reduction, for example—but also tension between national governments and the collectives they act for.

There is a problem of agency for ordinary people in this connected world: they act indirectly through their national citizenship and the problems are addressed as a matter of inter-state negotiation. There is often no way of directly electing people to represent a particular vision of global political economy at the geographical scale where action is required. Since the Cold War era this problem of agency has been addressed through sometimes impressive social movements: for nuclear disarmament, protection of the environment, or care for the human casualties of neo-liberal economics. While states cooperated over an international order, in other words, there was more coherent mobilization outside these institutions to influence their approach to increasingly shared transnational issues. This internationalism was partly a product of the increasing footprint (political, social, cultural, and ecological) of advanced economies, which made it harder to think

Figure 16. David Cameron and the Prince of Wales among world leaders at the signing of the Paris Climate Agreement in 2015

of environmental, humanitarian, and developmental issues as things unrelated to action in this part of the globe (Figure 16).

There has also been a domestic problem: that the ballot box does not seem to deliver effective agency—the power to remove governments is not the same as the power to meaningfully influence what they do. In the UK a two-party post-war consensus cultivated a sense that voting made little difference to real life. The combination of democracy with bureaucracy has limited the power to moderate or selectively implement national policies in the light of local realities.

British citizens entered this phase of global history as citizens of a medium-sized state with high GDP. Decolonization and relative economic decline dominated public discourse for much of the period from the 1960s to the 1990s, but the UK retained a relatively powerful position in inter-state organizations—as a nuclear power, a member of the UN Security Council, a G7 economy, and a major force in the commonwealth and the EU. Real wage growth stagnated for many ordinary people from the 1970s onwards, and mass unemployment in the 1980s gave way to fuller employment on less secure contracts—changes in the regulation of the labour market meant flexibility and increased insecurity. Nonetheless, and for all the talk of decline, GDP grew continuously and neoliberal political economy thrived as the explanation for that—denationalization, the reduction in union power, and a commitment to globalized free trade. This left local government with a relatively limited role—the UK is by European standards a highly centralized state—and declining turnouts for Westminster elections seemed to speak of political disengagement. The UK was responding to shared features of a global world—neoliberal globalization, proliferating inter-state cooperation, increasing mobility of capital (and latterly labour)—but its inhabitants had a particular experience of that shared history, which shaped their national citizenship.

* * *

This is of course a highly selective outline, but it is also instructive. It is based around the intertwining effects of material factors, institutional change, and ideas, none of them accounting for this history on its own. Opportunities for the powerful and the relatively powerless have shifted continuously and been played out in institutional battles shaped by the circumstances of the day, a process that can often be understood as a dialogue between collective and differential power. Over time, although not continuously, there has been an increase in global interdependence, and hence of the geographical scale over which collective institutions have acted for some purposes. This process is complex, but comprehensible. On Britain the outcome is the product of these political contests, chance, and the implications of decisions and institutional arrangements reached in particular circumstances which affected the future.

That distinctive path can at every point be understood as part of a broader shared experience, or as a parallel to the path taken in other global regions under pretty much the same pressures. In general, the widest scales of political life have been very significant—it has been here that changes in material conditions and influential ideas have moved, with implications for areas much larger than Great Britain. To understand broad patterns in political life on Great Britain it is usually necessary to place it in a global context—as part of a shared or parallel history. Importantly, though, in each of these phases there were also marked geographical contrasts between parts of Britain, as different parts of Britain connected with global developments in different ways. Other ways of dividing up this past are possible, but it is unlikely that they would escape these two very general conclusions.

In a way, then, this is ultimately a global history. At first sight that may seem paradoxical—that a history prompted by this one question (how have people used political power to get things done?) in relation to a single (albeit large) island could be a kind of global history. But writing that history constantly involves seeing the experience of a particular place in relation to much wider developments as either a parallel or shared experience, and usually with elements of both. A history of the globe should not be the only form for global history.

CONCLUSION

Globalizing the British Past: Parallel and Shared Histories

This book has covered a broader terrain than a more conventional British history tracing the origins of the UK and British identity. It has put people, power, and agency at the heart of political history in order to bring a broader range of past experience to bear on one of the central political questions of our age: how have the inhabitants of Great Britain used collective institutions to get things done?

National History in a Global Age

Writing about the political life of Great Britain over the long run is in some ways an eccentric thing to do. Historians have been increasingly drawn to writing global history in recent years, often through the history of connection—the movement of goods, ideas, or people, for example. This kind of writing is often an explicit alternative to national history (which still dominates much historical writing and teaching), and is in part a response to recent globalization. There are other reasons too why Great Britain may seem an odd unit to use for the history of political action over the long run. On one hand, few collective institutions have reached to all the coasts at once, and on the other, they have often reached other parts of the world while embracing only a part of the island. To put it most starkly, the United Kingdom has not yet lasted as long as the Kingdom of Wessex. There is little historical evidence that the island is a naturally self-contained and integrated political community.

Drawing attention to this fluidity runs counter to powerful conventions about the place of Britain in global history. A dominant view in the nineteenth and twentieth centuries was that as the first industrial democracy Britain had a special place in world history. This was an example of a wider, Eurocentric world history which saw the rise of the West in the nineteenth and twentieth centuries as inevitable, and much history (and other social science) set out to explain the features of Western life that accounted for this. Attacks on this global history—not least the observation that the rise of the West is likely to prove a phase in global development rather than a once-and-for-all endpoint—have tended therefore to reduce the global importance of British history.

In writing about political life *on* Britain I have not been trying to reclaim that place, but to give an example of another way of writing global history—how does the history of the globe look from this place?[1] The book argues for a general view of how collective power works, but also of how it has worked out in a particular region, and the narrative here could be compared with much of the rest of the globe in similar terms, revealing both parallels and shared experience. That is partly because these phases of development have so often been directly connected. Populations across Eurasia made some kind of adjustment to Rome and its rivals, while the impact of the Vikings was felt from the Black Sea to the eastern seaboard of North America. Dynastic interests connected the political life of the island with many other parts of Europe, as did long-distance trade, maritime empire, and recent globalization, disease, and technological change. Political ideas have rarely been contained within national borders and certainly not those that have driven major changes in patterns of collective action: Christianity, the renaissance, reformation, enlightenment, nationalism, communism, socialism, and neoliberalism (to name but a few). And where these things have not been directly connected, they have been paralleled—the organization of politics around dynasties, for example, was a feature of life across Eurasia, and societies with few direct connections have made parallel accommodations with new environmental or technological developments. Everywhere is unique, of course, but more as a variation on these shared and parallel experiences than as a matter of a peculiar national destiny based on character and institutional history.

These patterns in institutions, ideas, and material conditions have formed the shifting environment within which people living on Great Britain have tried to get things done—sometimes through these large institutional structures, sometimes more locally, and sometimes by mobilizing outside formal institutions. Only in the initial period of industrialization and the transition to mass democracy can developments on Britain be seen to be driving the wider process; in all other periods the population of the island was adjusting, accommodating, and taking advantage of developments arising from elsewhere. And in that period, when British industrialization and democratization led the world, it was of course a minority population on the island that was doing so, and who derived the principal benefits—as we have seen, during the 1890s 60 per cent of volunteers for military service from the richest island on the planet were deemed unfit to serve.

This is not to deny the significance of the nation states and national citizenship in the modern world, of course, but what to make of the nation state now presents something of a conundrum for both historians and politicians. Histories of global connection have left national history in an oddly marginal position given that for so many people their experience of that global history is heavily mediated by their national citizenship. The approach suggested here is that British institutions and identity are a product of the past that obviously matter in the present, but they are best understood as an outcome of path dependency within a broader global history, not as a natural and immutable destiny. Past circumstances, decisions, and chance have put the people of Great Britain in this relationship with the rest of the world. However, that citizenship and those national identities do not match, and are not the product of, the geography of the challenges they have faced or the resources they have had to define and meet them. People on the island have needed to act at larger and smaller scales too.

This bears on the key question posed throughout: what kinds of agency have been available to people living on Great Britain? That question becomes easier to answer as we approach our own time and the evidence becomes more abundant. However, we should not simply presume that greater visibility means that the actual scope for personal and collective agency has increased, or that it has done so continuously. For example, the freedoms we have enjoyed since the nineteenth century through the ballot box have been achieved alongside much closer bureaucratic regulation and surveillance—the *state* or *rule* of freedom as recent influential books have put it[2]—and at the expense of sharp exclusion for out-groups. At the same time, many people feel that nation states do not have the power to address material challenges operating at a global scale.

This book was prompted in part by the debate about what Global Britain might become. From the perspective adopted here, the key question is not about national identity or the powers of Westminster, but about what arrangements offer the best way to meet collective challenges. What matters is not so much how to be English, Scottish, Welsh, British, or European, or the sovereignty of the Westminster parliament, but rather what needs to be done and at what scale: for example, how to manage security, economy, environment, food, and epidemiology on an international scale, and what trade-offs are acceptable in handling other issues that do not require international action—education, many health services, road safety, food standards, and so on.

In that context a history with a disproportionate focus on sovereignty, Westminster, and national citizenship is unhelpful. Sovereignty, in fact, is an idea with a relatively recent history: it took off in the sixteenth century, in France, where a civil war led to the argument that political stability could only be achieved if a single source of authority was recognized as supreme. Jurisdiction is a much older and more flexible idea—the regulated power to achieve some particular purpose. In tackling twenty-first-century problems we may need to think more carefully about which collectives act, in what jurisdictions, and with what limitations. Rather than thinking exclusively about the sovereignty of nation states, we should think more flexibly about what needs to be done, by whom, and to whom they should answer. A history of political agency yields more food for thought in that context than a history of national institutions and identity.

A History for Use

If politics is the art of the possible, much public history and many politicians seem to have missed the point. Over the years UK politicians of all parties have placed more emphasis on understanding the history of British values and institutions than on the history of political agency. The priority has been to add to the pool of shared experience which knits us together as a political community.[3] For Gordon Brown, 'Citizenship is not an abstract concept, or just access to a passport. I believe it is—and must be seen as—founded on shared values that define the character of our country', while John Major hoped that 'Fifty years from now Britain will still be the country of long shadows on county grounds, warm beer, invincible green suburbs, dog lovers and pools fillers and—as George Orwell said—"old maids bicycling to Holy Communion through the morning mist" and if we get our way—Shakespeare still read even in school.'[4]

Statements like these two have often been prompted by discussion of migration or the EU, and in that context an understanding of the origins of Britain and Britishness has obvious political purposes. In fact and in fairness, Major's speech was mainly about getting things done in the light of the recently signed Maastricht treaty (1992) which set off a new round of European integration. He concluded with this (much-derided) quotation as a way of allaying fears that getting things done through the EU was a threat to Britishness (or here, more accurately, middle-class Southern Englishness): 'Britain will survive unamendable in all essentials.'[5] One influential response to this, important in contemporary politics, has been to criticize this view of Britishness as highly partial and selective—drawing attention to its blind spots in relation to the crimes and exclusions of the British past, and to the positive contribution made to collective life by those it leaves aside (by putting Mary Seacole alongside Florence Nightingale in the history of the Crimean War as taught in schools, for example).

The alternative presented here pays less attention to national identities partly because people have often acted in the name of groups smaller than the nation, or in groups not restricted to their own nation. Scottish people have acted locally—as Glaswegians, for example—or transnationally—as peace activists—but have also fought for, benefited from, and contributed to the harm caused by the British empire. To get things done we act in more than one collective group, often at the same time, and have more than one potential political identity.

Moreover, identities are powerful ideas that are themselves shaped by institutional contexts—it is easier to act as a Glaswegian than as a woman, for example, because there are strong collective institutions in place to act on Glaswegian interests. In fact, institutions to some extent create collective identities—as we have seen in relation to both ninth-century England and eighteenth-century Britain. The rise of the EU had helped foster collective identities among Britons that became entrenched in the Brexit debates—Brexiteer or Remainer were descriptions of a set of (assumed) values and beliefs, not simply a description of a voting preference in relation to a set of institutional relationships.

There is a broader history of collective institutions to be understood and learned from than the story of the UK and its associated identity. Seeing the past in terms of a linear development towards a natural condition in the present limits our understanding by offering a 'teleology': it gives an explanation for the present which assumes it is a necessary outcome of past development, and therefore directs us into the future as if on railway tracks. A more fluid view of the shifting possibilities of collective life in the past keeps alive the memory not just of how we got here but also of how things have been different, or might have been. A broader understanding of the past gives a less narrow view of the present and a less limiting view of the possibilities for the future.

* * *

Professional historians argue not just about the accuracy of our accounts of the past but also about the coherence of our explanations for what has happened. That can mean trying to unpick in detail the relationship between ideas and material change, or between political and economic power in shaping historical development. These interpretive issues are also important for active politicians: does political intervention improve economic and social life or not? Will climate change issues be resolved by the market? Historical writing is innately political in fact because it is structured, consciously or unconsciously, by views about these relationships.

The view taken here on fundamental methodological issues has been relatively neutral: that in explaining the uses of collective institutions we cannot consistently allocate primacy to ideas, material change, or organizational structures. The effects of Rome on the island seem to demonstrate the power of institutions, the growth of inter-governmental action in the post-war period demonstrates the effects of economic and environmental forces, changes in Anglo-Saxon law codes the power of new ideas about how the world works. In reality, as has been clear in every case, political action results from the interaction of all three, and so, for example, the power of ideas depends on the material and institutional environment—neoliberal or Keynesian ideas would have been of little use to the Vikings. For the same reason, though, we cannot consider ideas in isolation. Neoliberalism is no less a product of its historical context than ideals of courtly love and chivalry were in the eleventh century.

In that context this book has described more than it has explained. It has aimed only to set out an anatomy of how political power has worked, and to put some flesh on the bones with historical examples. Collective institutions allow us to manage our world but also each other. They both create and restrain differential power, formalizing the restraint in charters, elections, or inter-governmental agreements, but also putting kings and a disproportionate number of old Etonians in positions of authority. Ideas determine the form and content of these agreements, which are also made in the face of real and material challenges. What collective institutions do, and how they are regulated, sets the limits for what is possible in the future. They act at different geographical scales—in the case of Great Britain, at imperial, Western, European, national, regional, and local levels, for example. Each one reflects but also cements the existence of a collective. Different identities are expressed in these institutional settlements, but these settlements themselves foster those shared identities. All these relationships are reciprocal rather than unidirectional: between collective and differential power, between collective institutions and identity, and between collective institutions and ideas, economic behaviour, or technological change.

By describing these relationships, this book invites the reader to think about agency in a fuller historical perspective and explore further what historians have made of these relationships at various times and in various places. Reading about the past with critical contemporary questions in mind helps to clarify our own view of the political world: even those who hate politics have a theory of it.

Although attempting neutrality on these methodological and ideological issues, this is in another way a very political book, however. Taking this very long view, there is no particular reason to think we have reached an endpoint in institutional development, or that any point of equilibrium reached in the past was the natural one that should be recovered. A history that gives us a fuller sense of how people have exercised agency in the past (often outside and beyond Westminster and acting not just on Great Britain) should help us think more flexibly about how to achieve it now and in the future. Politics is fundamentally about maximizing our collective power to take control over the material and social world while restraining the harmful effects of differential power on our individual and collective lives. This book has not proposed an answer, or offered an institutional blueprint, but rather offered an invitation to have a different and more productive discussion about what past experience might teach us.

NOTES

Introduction

1. https://en.wikipedia.org/wiki/List_of_islands_by_area (accessed 14 July 2020).
2. K. Marx, *The Eighteenth Brumaire of Louis Napoleon* (1852) https://www.marxists.org/archive/marx/works/1852/18th-brumaire/ch01.htm (accessed 14 July 2020).

Chapter 1

1. B. Campbell, *The Romans and Their World* (2011), ch. 1.
2. G. De La Bédouyère, *The Real Lives of Roman Britain* (2016), pp. 8–10.
3. Ibid., p. 34.
4. A. King and I. Crewe, *The Blunders of Our Governments* (2013), ch. 2, 'An array of successes'.
5. N. Higham and M. J. Ryan (eds), *The Anglo-Saxon World* (2013), p. 345.
6. D. Pratt, 'Demesne exemption from royal taxation in Anglo-Saxon and Anglo-Norman England', *English Historical Review,* 128 (2013); D. Pratt, 'Charters and exemption from geld in Anglo-Saxon England', in R. Naismith and D. A. Woodman (eds), *Writing, Kingship and Power in Anglo-Saxon England* (2018). For taxation and consent see J. R. Maddicott, *The Origins of the English Parliament, 924–1327* (Oxford, 2010).
7. C. Wickham, *Medieval Europe* (2017), p. 151.
8. M. Braddick, 'Case of ship-money (*R v Hampden*) (1637): Prerogatival discretion in emergency conditions', in D. de Cogan and J. Snape (eds), *Landmark Cases in Revenue Law* (2018).
9. The case is discussed in G. R. Rubin, *Private Property, Government Requisition and the Constitution, 1914–27* (1994), ch. 6.
10. E. A. Wrigley, 'A simple model of London's importance in changing English society and economy, 1650–1750', *Past and Present,* 37 (1967).
11. H. Mayhew, *London Labour and the London Poor* (1864/5 edn), vol. 2, pp. 510–11. It was a matter of regret to Mayhew that this was seen primarily as a problem of waste disposal, rather than the recycling of a valuable fertilizer: pp. 437–9. For use by market gardeners around

London in the later eighteenth century see E. Cockayne, *Hubbub: Filth, Noise, and Stench in England, 1600–1770* (2007), p. 93. Asian cities were much more systematic in their recycling of Human waste for agriculture: D. T. Ferguson, 'Nightsoil and the "Great Divergence": Human waste, the urban economy, and economic productivity, 1500–1900', *Journal of Global History*, 9 (2014).

12. A number of historians have written with relish about these sanitary issues in London: P. Ackroyd, *London: The Biography* (2001), ch. 36; S. Halliday, *The Great Stink of London* (1999); P. Dobraszczyk, *London's Sewers* (2014). See, more generally, Cockayne, *Hubbub*.

13. F. Sheppard, *London: A History* (1998), pp. 280–2.

14. P. T. Marsh, 'Chamberlain, Joseph (1836–1914)', *ODNB* (paywall).

15. J. Vernon, *Modern Britain: 1750 to the Present* (2017), pp. 373–5. For arguments against nationalization and examples of successful privatization see King and Crewe, *Blunders*, pp. 15–16.

Chapter 2

1. C. Wickham, *Framing the Middle Ages* (2005), pp. 47–50.

2. A. Taylor, *The Shape of the State in Medieval Scotland, 1124–1290* (2016).

3. B. Cunliffe, *Britain Begins* (2012), esp. pp. 198–9. It does seem that it was new people and not just new ideas: D. Reich, *Who We Are and How We Got Here* (2018), pp. 114–17.

4. Cited from P. Salway, 'Roman Britain', in K. Morgan (ed.), *The Oxford History of Britain* (1988), pp. 20–1.

5. N. Higham and M. J. Ryan, *The Anglo-Saxon World* (2013), esp. p. 145.

6. D. J. Tyler, 'Offa's Dyke: A historiographical appraisal', *Journal of Medieval History* (2011); P. Squatriti, 'Digging ditches in early medieval Europe', *Past and Present* (2002). Mercian kings may have fostered the growth and fortification of towns as an assertion of royal authority too: S. Bassett, 'Divide and rule? The military infrastructure of eighth- and ninth-century Mercia', *Early Medieval Europe* (2007).

7. T. Lambert, *Law and Order in Anglo-Saxon England* (Oxford, 2017). See also J. Hudson, *The Formation of the English Common Law* (2nd edn, 2018), ch. 3.

8. Lambert, *Law and Order*; L. Roach, 'Penance, submission and *deditio*: Religious influences on dispute settlement in later Anglo-Saxon England (871–1066)', *Anglo-Saxon England*, 41 (2012); Roach, 'Law codes and legal norms in later Anglo-Saxon England', *Historical Research*, 86:233 (2013).

9. https://www.oxforddnb.com (paywall).
10. P. Slack, *The Invention of Improvement* (2015).
11. M. Ogborn, *Spaces of Modernity: London's Geographies 1680–1780* (1998). For the other examples in this and the following two paragraphs see J. Vernon, *Modern Britain: 1750 to the Present* (2017).
12. K. Raworth, *Doughnut Economics* (2017), pp. 36–8.
13. For this argument see Q. Skinner, 'Some problems in the analysis of political thought and action', reprinted in J. Tully (ed.), *Meaning and Context: Quentin Skinner and His Critics* (1988).
14. Navigation Act quoted from https://www.constitution.org/eng/con-pur_ap.htm, accessed 19 August 2019.
15. B. Worden, *The Rump Parliament, 1649–1653* (1974), ch. 11, esp. pp. 232–4, ch. 14.
16. K. Thomas, 'The puritans and adultery: The Act of 1650 reconsidered', in D. Pennington and K. Thomas (eds), *Puritans and Revolutionaries* (1978).
17. St Phillip's Settlement Education and Research Society, *The Equipment of the Workers* (1919).
18. http://antipolitics.soton.ac.uk/files/2014/10/The-rise-of-anti-politics-in-Britain.pdf, accessed 18 July 2019.
19. S. Walker, 'Rumour, sedition and popular protest in the reign of Henry IV', *Past and Present* (2000); D. Cressy, *Dangerous Talk* (2010).
20. W. A. Speck, *Stability and Strife: England 1714–1760* (1977), pp. 256–7.
21. J. S. Mill, *Considerations on Representative Government* (1861), ch. 7, 'Of true and false democracy; representation of all, and representation of the majority only'.

Chapter 3

1. It is important to say that we can learn a lot about the development of cognition from material culture and there is now a fascinating and rapidly developing literature on the evolution of the mind: S. Mithen, *The Prehistory of the Mind* (1998), Mithen, *The Singing Neanderthals* (2006), C. Renfrew, *Prehistory: The Making of the Human Mind* (2007), C. Gamble, J. Gowlett, and R. Dunbar, *Thinking Big: How the Evolution of Social Life Shaped the Human Mind* (2014). The point here is that we can tell very little about the specific content of abstract and symbolic thinking about collective life until much later periods: we know that humans were

capable of that *kind* of thought, but we know very little about the detail of *what* they thought.

2. J. C. Scott, *Against the Grain: A Deep History of the Earliest States* (2017). For an earlier questioning of the relationship between agriculture and the state see M. Mann, *The Sources of Social Power*, vol. 1 (1986), ch. 2.

3. Göbekli Tepe in modern Turkey is one such, discussed in S. Mithen, *After the Ice* (2004), pp. 65–7. It may be that settlement clustered around a ritual site at Çatalhöyük, perhaps prompting rather than resulting from farming: I. Hodder, *Çatalhöyük: The Leopard's Tale—Revealing the Mysteries of Turkey's Ancient 'Town'* (2006), pp. 234–5, 243–5. There, however, archaeologists are analysing one of the earliest accumulations of domestic dwellings in a town rather than the construction of a large collective project.

4. M. J. Braddick, 'Noell, Sir Martin (bap. 1614, d. 1665)' and Braddick, 'Fox, Sir Stephen (1627–1716)', in *The Oxford Dictionary of National Biography* https://www.oxforddnb.com (paywall). For the relationship between London mercantile wealth and the development of Barbados see M. D. Bennett, 'Merchant capital and the origins of the Barbados sugar boom, 1627–1672', Unpublished PhD thesis, University of Sheffield, 2019.

5. M. Ogborn, *Global Lives: Britain and the World, 1550–1800* (2008).

6. For an overview and a critical commentary on the idea of the Anthropocene based on the need to integrate individual and collective agency into our picture, see A. Malm and A. Hornborg, 'The geology of mankind? A critique of the Anthropocene narrative', *The Anthropocene Review*, I (2014).

7. P. Clavin, *Securing the World Economy: The Reinvention of the League of Nations, 1920–1946* (2013).

8. N. Draper, 'Slavery and Britain's infrastructure', Legacies of British Slave-ownership project blog, https://lbsatucl.wordpress.com, accessed 19 August 2019.

9. G. Parker, *Global Crisis: War, Climate Change and Catastrophe in the Seventeenth Century* (2013).

10. F. Pryor, *The Making of the British Landscape* (2010), pp. 98–9.

11. T. Johnson, 'The tree and the rod: Jurisdiction in late medieval England', *Past and Present* (2017).

12. R. A. Dodgshon, 'The Little Ice Age in the Scottish Highlands and Island: Documenting its human impact', *Scottish Geographical Journal*, 121 (2005).

13. D. Levine and K. Wrightson, *The Making of an Industrial Society: Whickham 1560–1765* (1991), quotation at pp. 111–12.

14. W. Cavert, *The Smoke of London: Energy and Environment in the Early Modern City* (2016), p. 234; King and Crewe, *Blunders*, pp. 10–11.

15. C. Bonneuil and J.-P. Fressoz, *The Shock of the Anthropocene* (English translation, 2016), ch. 5.

16. J. W. S. Longhurst et al., 'Acid deposition: A select review 1852–1990', *Fuel*, 72:9 (1993).

17. http://www.unece.org/env/lrtap/welcome.html.html, accessed 19 August 2019; https://unfccc.int/resource/docs/2015/cop21/eng/l09r01.pdf, accessed 19 August 2019.

18. M. Clanchy, *From Memory to Written Record* (3rd edition, 2012).

19. M. Ogborn, *Indian Ink: Script and Print in the Making of the English East India Company* (2007).

20. N. Tadmor, 'Settlement of the poor and the rise of the form in England, c. 1662–1780', *Past and Present* (2017).

21. Vernon, *Modern Britain*, pp. 116–21, 141, 290; E. Higgs, *The Information State in England* (2004), ch. 4.

22. M. Howard, *War in European History* (1976).

23. One online calculator gives the value in relative purchasing power as £163.4 m, with three other ways of doing the sum producing a range of results from £147.5 m to £80 bn: https://www.measuringworth.com/calculators/ukcompare.

24. The classic study, now much debated and extended, is G. Parker, *The Military Revolution* (1988).

25. A. J. P. Taylor, *English History, 1914–1945* (1965), p. 1; D. Edgerton, *Warfare State: Britain, 1920–1950* (2005).

Chapter 4

1. R. Smith, 'Contrasting susceptibility to famine in early fourteenth- and late sixteenth-century England', in M. J. Braddick and P. Withington (eds), *Popular Culture and Political Agency in Early Modern England and Ireland* (2017).

2. A. Sen, *Poverty and Famines* (1981).

3. J. Walter, 'The social economy of dearth in early modern England', in J. Walter and R. Schofield (eds), *Famine, Disease and the Social Order in Early Modern Society* (1989).

4. Smith, 'Contrasting susceptibility'.

5. P. Slack, *The Impact of Plague in Tudor and Stuart England* (1985); B. Bramanti et al., 'The third plague pandemic in Europe', *Proceedings of the Royal Society*, 286 (2019).

6. K. Wrightson, *Ralph Tailor's Summer* (2011).

7. Slack, *Plague*, pp. 268–9; M. J. Braddick, *State Formation in Early Modern England* (2000), pp. 126–7.

8. https://www.who.int/en/news-room/fact-sheets/detail/plague, accessed 23 July 2019.

9. http://www.wpro.who.int/entity/drug_resistance/resources/global_action_plan_eng.pdf, accessed 19 August 2019.

10. A. King and I. Crewe, *The Blunders of Our Governments* (2013), pp. 19–20.

11. https://www.bbc.co.uk/news/world-52103747, accessed 8 April 2020.

12. https://royalsocietypublishing.org/doi/10.1098/rspb.2019.2736, accessed 8 April 2020; https://www.bbc.co.uk/news/science-environment-52369878, accessed 16 April 2021; https://www.bbc.co.uk/news/uk-56713388, accessed 16 April 2021; https://www.bbc.co.uk/news/uk-56572775, accessed 16 April, 2021.

13. P. Salway, 'Roman Britain', in K. Morgan (ed.), *Oxford History of Britain* (1988); G. De La Bédouyère, *The Real Lives of Roman Britain* (2016), ch. 3; R. Fleming, *Britain after Rome* (2010), ch. 1.

14. G. R. Fincham, 'Military communications in the East Anglian fenland during the Roman period', *Papers from the Institute of Archaeology*, 9 (1998).

15. Salway, 'Roman Britain'; De La Bédouyère, *Real Lives*, ch. 3.

16. M. Millett, *Roman Britain* (1995), ch. 1; I. D. Whyte, *Scotland before the Industrial Revolution* (1995), ch. 4.

17. C. Wickham, *Framing the Middle Ages* (2005), pp. 47–50; B. Ward-Perkins, *The Fall of Rome* (2005) also sees Britain as a particularly dramatic example of collapse (see, for example, Benedict, p. 108). J. Gerard, *The Ruin of Britain* (2013) gives a more gradualist account.

18. F. Sheppard, *London: A History* (1998), ch. 4.

19. Whyte, *Scotland*, chs 2, 4. For David's place in the broader development of Scottish government in the high middle ages see A. Taylor, *The Shape of the State in Medieval Scotland, 1124–1290* (Oxford, 2016).

20. C. Briggs, *Credit and Village Society in Fourteenth-Century England* (2009); C. Muldrew, *The Economy of Obligation* (1998); T. Paul, *The Poverty of Disaster: Debt and Insecurity in Eighteenth-Century Britain* (2019).

21. J. Vernon, *Modern Britain: 1750 to the Present* (2017), pp. 493–4.

22. J. Lanchester, *Whoops!* (2010); for CDSs and regulation see esp. ch. 2 and pp. 156–8.

23. Vernon, *Modern Britain*, p. 135.
24. J. H. Baker, *An Introduction to English Legal History* (4th edition, 2000), ch. 2.
25. D. Underdown, *Fire from Heaven* (1992).
26. J. H. Elliott, 'Atlantic history: A circumnavigation', in D. Armitage and M. J. Braddick (eds), *The British Atlantic World* (2nd edition, 2009), pp. 241–3.

Chapter 5

1. https://www.bbc.co.uk/news/magazine-12244964, accessed 25 April 2019.
2. R. Naismith, 'The currency of power in late Anglo-Saxon England', *History Compass*, 17 (2019).
3. E. Duffy, *The Stripping of the Altars* (2005), pp. 38–40.
4. C. Phythian Adams, 'Ritual constructions of society', in R. Horrox and W. M. Ormrod (eds), *A Social History of England, 1200–1500* (2006); R. Hutton, *The Rise and Fall of Merry England: The Ritual Year 1400–1700* (1994).
5. J. Kent, 'Population mobility and alms', *Local Population Studies*, 27 (1981); S. Hindle, *On the Parish?* (2004), ch. 5; N. Tadmor, *The Settlement of the Poor in England* (2020).
6. For Birmingham and Glasgow see T. Hunt, *Building Jerusalem* (2004), ch. 8.
7. St Phillip's Settlement Education and Research Society, *The Equipment of the Workers* (1919), p. 69.
8. A. King and I. Crewe, *The Blunders of Our Governments* (2013), p. 44.
9. R. Frame, *The Political Development of the British Isles 1100–1400* (1990).
10. A. Iriye, *Global Community: The Role of International Organisations in the Making of the Contemporary World* (2004). For the reform of global institutions see, for example, J. E. Stiglitz, *Making Globalization Work* (2006); and I. Goldin, *Divided Nations* (2013).
11. K. Kumar, *The Making of English National Identity* (2003); L. Colley, *Britons: Forging the Nation, 1707–1837* (1992).
12. D. Cannadine, 'The context, performance and meaning of ritual', in E. Hobsbawm and T. Ranger (eds), *The Invention of Tradition* (1983), p. 125.
13. R. Vinen, *National Service: A Generation in Uniform, 1945–63* (2015).
14. J. Hoppit, *Britain's Political Economies* (2017).
15. D. Goodhart, *The Road to Somewhere* (2017) relates these identity issues to the failures of collective institutions to embrace all constituencies effectively.

Chapter 6

1. Ordinance of 24 October 1644, https://www.british-history.ac.uk/no-series/acts-ordinances-interregnum/pp554-555, accessed 18 September 2019.
2. A. Rio, *Slavery after Rome, 500–1100* (Oxford, 2017).
3. J. R. Walkowitz and D. J. Walkowitz, '"We are not beasts of the field": Prostitution and the poor in Plymouth and Southampton under the Contagious Diseases Act', *Feminist Studies*, 1 (1973). For sus laws see, for example, http://news.bbc.co.uk/1/hi/uk/6696229.stm, accessed 21 August 2019; https://www.theguardian.com/uk-news/2018/nov/13/knife-crime-stop-and-search-and-violence-as-entertainment, accessed 21 August 2019; and for the longer history see J. Miller, 'The touch of the state: Stop and search in England, c.1660–1750', *HistoryWorkshop Journal*, 87 (2019).
4. For this argument see Q. Skinner, 'Some problems in the analysis of political thought and action' reprinted in J. Tully (ed.), *Meaning and Context: Quentin Skinner and His Critics* (1988).
5. J. Walter and K. Wrightson, 'Dearth and the social order in early modern England', *Past and Present*, 71 (1976).
6. https://www.theguardian.com/theguardian/2007/apr/27/great-speeches, accessed 24 April 2019.
7. Quoted in M. J. Braddick, 'State formation and political culture in Elizabethan and Stuart England', in R. Asch and D. Freist (eds), *Staatsbildung als kultereller prozess* (2005).
8. K. Lindley, *Popular Politics and Religion in Civil War London* (1997), pp. 134–6.
9. A. McKenzie, 'Martyrs in low life? Dying "game" in Augustan England', *Journal of British Studies*, 42 (2003).
10. S. Justice, *Writing and Rebellion: England in 1381* (1996).
11. J. Watts, *The Making of Polities: Europe 1300–1500* (2009).
12. P. Earle, *Monmouth's Rebels* (1978).
13. C. Brooks, *Lawyers, Litigation and English Society* (p. 2 for the importance of his memory of civil rights).
14. For the general point see E. P. Thompson, *Customs in Common* (1991) (which has inspired many others), and for the defeat of governments in the period after 1790 see P. Harling, 'The law of libel and the limits of repression', *Historical Journal*, 44 (2001).
15. S. J. Watts and S. J. Watts, *From Border to Middle Shire* (1974); A. Groundwater, *The Scottish Middle March* (2013).
16. D. Whitten, 'The Don Pacifico affair', *The Historian*, 48 (1986).

17. D. Rollison, *A Commonwealth of the People: Popular Politics and England's Long Social Revolution, 1066–1649* (2010); A. Wood, *The 1549 Rebellions and the Making of Early Modern England* (2006).

18. Quoted in D. Norbrook, *Poetry and Politics in the English Renaissance* (2002), p. 142.

19. J. Watts, 'The pressure of the public on later medieval politics', in L. Clark and C. Carpenter (eds), *Political Culture in Later Medieval England* (2004); Watts, 'Public or plebs: The changing meaning of "the commons", 1381–1549', in H. Pryce and J. Watts (eds), *Power and Identity in the Middle Ages* (2007).

20. https://www.theguardian.com/law/2010/nov/29/mangrove-nine-40th-anniversary, accessed 25 April 2019.

21. G. De La Bédouyère, *The Real Lives of Roman Britain* (2016), pp. 114, 117; B. Cunliffe, *Britain Begins* (2012), p. 373.

22. J. Gillingham, 'Conquests, catastrophe and recovery', in J. C. D. Clark (ed.), *A World by Itself* (2010), p. 116.

23. M. Kaufmann, *Black Tudors* (2017), chs 1, 3; D. Olusoga, *Black and British* (2017), pp. 16–17, 59–61.

24. K. Kupperman, *Pocahontas and the English Boys* (2019).

25. P. Moore, *Endeavour: The Ship and the Attitude that Changed the World* (2018), N. Thomas, *Discoveries: The Voyages of Captain Cook* (2003), p. 314. I am grateful to John Moreland for this reference.

26. Olusoga, *Black and British*, pp. 19–20.

27. C. L. R. James, *Beyond a Boundary* (1963). Constantine was later to become very politically active.

28. J. Peacey and C. R. Kyle (eds), *Parliament at Work* (2002); A. Vickery, 'The political day in London, c. 1679–1834', *Past and Present* (forthcoming).

29. N. Karn, 'Centralism and local government in medieval England', *History Compass*, 10 (2012).

30. D. Eastwood, *Government and Community in the English Provinces, 1700–1870* (Basingstoke, 1997).

31. A. King and I. Crewe, *The Blunders of Our Governments* (2013), pp. 17–18.

32. Olusoga, *Black and British*, esp. p. 28.

Chapter 7

1. For a comprehensive view of the importance of the fourteenth century from an ecological perspective see B. M. S. Campbell, *The Great Transformation* (2016).

2. I. Forrest, *Trustworthy Men: How Inequality and Faith Made the Medieval Church* (2018).
3. P. Slack, *From Reformation to Improvement* (1998).

Conclusion

1. M. Haneda, *Toward Creation of a New World History* (2018).
2. P. Joyce, *The Rule of Freedom* (2003); Joyce, *The State of Freedom* (2013).
3. For the politics of Englishness in this context see P. Mandler, *The English National Character: The History of an Idea from Edmund Burke to Tony Blair* (2006).
4. Brown was speaking in the context of proposals for 'managed migration and earned citizenship', quoted in J. Bate, 'The use and abuse of national history and the national poet', in J. Bate (ed.), *The Public Value of the Humanities* (2011), p. 56; John Major, speech to Conservative Group for Europe, 22 April 1993, http://www.johnmajorarchive.org.uk/1990-1997/mr-majors-speech-to-conservative-group-for-europe-22-april-1993, accessed 20 August 2019.
5. Major, speech to Conservative Group for Europe.

PICTURE CREDITS

FURTHER READING

History books tend to have a single name on them but are the result of collaboration and conversation with many others, and this book certainly relies on the work of many other people. However, the examples I use rely on knowledge accumulated over three decades of teaching British history, so that it is not always easy to acknowledge a particular source or colleague. I hope that my academic colleagues will forgive me if their own original contribution has been overlooked or subsumed in a more general reference: my priority here has been to offer guides to further reading for non-experts.

An interested reader could find out more about particular examples or episodes in this book from many standard works or reliable online sources. For more detailed description and discussion of the archaeological sites mentioned here the English Heritage websites are often very informative, as is F. Pryor, *Britain BC: Life in Britain Before the Romans* (2003). Books on particular periods that I have relied on to update my knowledge or for accurate detail include: C. Stringer, *Homo Britannicus: The Incredible Story of Human Life in Britain* (2006), B. Cunliffe, *Britain Begins* (2012) [covering the archaeology of Britain and Ireland from the period from human settlement up to the Norman conquest], K. Morgan (ed.), *Oxford History of Britain* (1988), J. C. D. Clark (ed.), *A World by Itself* (2010), B. Campbell, *The Romans and Their World* (2011), G. De La Bédouyère, *The Real Lives of Roman Britain* (2016), M. Millett, *Roman Britain* (1995),

C. Wickham, *The Inheritance of Rome* (2009), R. Fleming, *Britain after Rome* (2010), N. Higham and M. J. Ryan, *The Anglo-Saxon World* (2013), R. Frame, *The Political Development of the British Isles, 1100–1400* (1990), D. Walker, *Medieval Wales* (1990), I. D. Whyte, *Scotland before the Industrial Revolution* (1995), A. D. M. Barrell, *Medieval Scotland* (2000), J. Watts, *The Making of Polities: Europe 1300–1500* (2009), B. M. S. Campbell, *The Great Transformation* (2016) [fourteenth century], M. Lynch, *Scotland: A New History* (1992 edn), J. Vernon, *Modern Britain: 1750 to the Present* (2017), and K. O'Rourke, *A Short History of Brexit: From Brentry to Brexit* (2018).

For recent globalization and inter- and supra-state organizations see A. Iriye, *Global Community: The Role of International Organisations in the Making of the Contemporary World* (2004) and M. Mazower, *Governing the World: The History of an Idea* (2013). For social history and issues of inclusion and exclusion, M. Cook and R. Mills, *A Gay History of Britain* (2007), D. Olusoga, *Black and British* (2017), J. Crick and E. van Houts (eds), *A Social History of England 900–1200* (2011), R. Horrox and W. M. Ormrod (eds), *A Social History of England, 1200–1500* (2006), and K. Wrightson (ed.), *A Social History of England 1500–1750* (2017). For an overview of historical arguments about globalization see P. N. Stearns, *Globalization in World History* (2nd edn, 2016), J. Osterhammel, *The Transformation of the World: A Global History of the Nineteenth Century* (2014), N. P. Petersson, *Globalization: A Short History* (English translation, 2005), and S. Conrad, *What Is Global History?* (2016).

Introduction

For collective and distributive (here 'differential') power see M. Mann, *The Sources of Social Power*, vol. 1 (1986), ch. 1. For the self-organizing economy see P. Krugman, *The Self-Organising*

Economy (1995). There it has a much more technical meaning, taking theories of self-organizing complex systems developed in the natural sciences and using them to understand how the economy works. It is also a controversial idea, since many people think that without political intervention economic systems tend to fail. Hence my phrase 'in principle': in practice, as we see throughout the book, economic and political organization intertwine. I use the term more loosely and in a non-technical sense to mean simply the undirected actions of individuals which generate interdependence: I do not try to develop an analysis of the dynamics of such systems.

As I suggest in the text, 'agency' is a similarly complex notion in academic writing. It may seem to assume, for example, that we can really know our own mind, and then act rationally based on that knowledge. Are either of these things actually true, though? Our apparent desires and actions can be the product of unconscious impulses, manipulated by others or simply an expression of collectively held values and expectations passing through us as we conform to the expectations of others. Moreover, some analyses assume that many, perhaps most, of our drives are genetic rather than conscious or rational. And even if we think our apparent motives represent rational and accurate knowledge of our own individual interests, in such a 'rational choice' view of human action what 'we' need to do is often dictated from outside ourselves, perhaps even consciously so by vested interests. For all these and other reasons, Kristian Kristiansen questions whether it is useful to think about agency at all in archaeological contexts, wondering whether it is not simply a narcissistic conceit of the twentieth century: we want to believe that we are rational individual actors and are simply projecting that on to the past. He prefers terms for specific kinds of action, many of which describe the kind of agency I am exploring here such as 'power, manipulation, exploitation, opposition and resistance' (Kristiansen, 'Genes versus agents: A discussion of the widening theoretical gap in archaeology', *Archaeological Dialogues* (2004)).

In this book I am simply trying to show that people have acted collectively to exert greater influence over the material and social conditions of their existence. That is a much smaller claim than that individuals and groups have acquired full autonomy and freedom, or that they have used politics to achieve their own flourishing. However, although this is a less fundamental question, it is not a trivial one—collective action has sometimes profoundly improved the conditions in which individuals and groups make their lives. Fourteenth-century peasants might not have been able to make much sense of a modern notion of agency, and it is almost certainly true that they did not use political power to achieve a full and individual human flourishing. We do know, however, that they could act collectively to try to improve the conditions of their existence.

Chapter 1

In addition to the relevant general works above see, for the later development of land taxes, M. Jurkowski et al., *Lay Taxes in England and Wales, 1188–1688* (1998) and, for the transformation of state finances and its consequences during the seventeenth century, M. Braddick, 'The rise of the fiscal state', in Barry Coward (ed.), *A Companion to Stuart Britain* (2002). For London's growth and urban history more generally see P. Clark (ed.), *The Cambridge Urban History of Britain*, vol. II 1540–1840 (2000). Among the many studies of the EU I have found R. Bootle, *The Trouble with Europe* (2015 edn) and O'Rourke (above) very helpful.

CHAPTER 2

In addition to the relevant general works listed above see, for the impact of Christianity on Anglo-Saxon life, J. Blair, *The Church in Anglo-Saxon Society* (2005). For 'reformation politics' see J. Scott, *England's Troubles* (2000) and for the reformation in Scotland see A. Ryrie, *The Origins of the Scottish Reformation* (2006). The fate of Protestantism in Ireland is a matter of ongoing debate. For a recent contribution and further references see H. A. Jefferies, 'Why the Reformation failed in Ireland', *Irish Historical Studies*, 40 (2016). For statistical thinking see J. C. Scott, *Seeing Like a State* (1998), and A. W. Crosby, *The Measure of Reality: Quantification in Western Europe, 1250–1600* (1997). For probabilistic thinking see B. J. Shapiro, *Probability and Certainty in Seventeenth-Century England* (1983), I. Hacking, *The Emergence of Probability* (1975), and R. H. Popkin, *The History of Scepticism* (3rd edn, 2003). For neoliberalism see D. Harvey, *A Brief History of Neoliberalism* (2007).

CHAPTER 3

In addition to the relevant general works listed above see, for the wider Viking world, P. Parker, *The Northmen's Fury* (2015). For the opening up of Atlantic trade and the origins of the British empire see N. Canny (ed.), *The Oxford History of the British Empire*, vol. I, *The Origins of Empire* (1998). For globalization and the power of international and inter-governmental institutions see J. E. Stiglitz, *Making Globalization Work* (2006) and I. Goldin, *Divided Nations* (2013).

CHAPTER 4

In addition to the relevant general works listed above see, for the development of English local government, A. R. Brown, *The Governance of Late Medieval England* (1989), A. G. R. Smith, *The Government of Elizabethan England* (1967), and P. Williams, *The Tudor Regime* (1979). For the Scottish contrast see W. Makey, *The Church of the Covenant* (1979) and J. Goodare, *The Government of Scotland, 1560–1625* (2004).

CHAPTER 5

For local government, in addition to Brown, Smith, Williams (above), see D. Eastwood, *Government and Community in the English Provinces, 1700–1870* (1997) and T. Hunt, *Building the New Jerusalem: The Rise and Fall of the Victorian City* (2006). For dynastic politics in comparative global context see J. Duindam, *Dynasties: A Global History of Power, 1300–1800* (2015). For the empire see J. Darwin, *Unfinished Empire: The Global Expansion of Britain* (2012) and Darwin, *The Empire Project* (2010). For twentieth-century globalization, institutional development, and political agency of ordinary people see S. Pedersen, *The Guardians: The League of Nations and the Crisis of Empire* (2017) and P. Clavin, *Securing the World Economy: The Reinvention of the League of Nations, 1920–1946* (2013), as well as Mazower (above).

CHAPTER 6

In addition to the general works above see, for the poor law, P. Slack, *Poverty and Policy in Tudor and Stuart England* (1988) and S. Hindle, *On the Parish?* (2004). For civil war radicalism, John Lilburne and petitioning: M. Braddick, *The Common Freedom of the People* (2018). For formalization of jurisdiction between the thirteenth and fifteenth centuries see E. Hartrich, *Politics and the Urban Sector in Fifteenth-Century England* (2019), and for boroughs in the later period P. Withington, *The Politics of Commonwealth* (2009). For petitioning see D. Zaret, *The Origins of Democratic Culture* (2000). For life at the margins see J. C. Scott, *The Art of Not Being Governed* (2011). For the modern nation as an 'imagined community' see B. Anderson, *Imagined Communities* (1983). For sexual subcultures see R. Norton, *Mother Clap's Molly House* (1992) and C. Mounsey and C. Gonda, *Queer People: Negotiations and Expressions of Homosexuality, 1700–1800* (2007), and for alehouses see M. Hailwood, *Alehouses and Good Fellowship in Early Modern England* (2014).

CHAPTER 7

This chapter mainly presents material already discussed and can be followed up through the general works listed above.

CONCLUSION

For reflections on the complexity and continuing importance of national identities in a globalized context see A. Burton (ed.), *After the Imperial Turn: Thinking With and Through the Nation* (2003). For the role of national citizenship see P. G. Cerny, 'Globalization and the changing logic of collective action', *International Organization*, 49 (1995). For the nation state and globalization see U. Hedetoft, *The Global Turn: National Encounters with the World* (2003). The academic field of International Political Economy also pays sustained attention to the nation state as an actor in global affairs: see B. J. Cohen, *Advanced Introduction to International Political Economy* (2014). Seabrooke has drawn attention to the agency of national citizens in this international political economy; for example, L. Seabrooke, 'Everyday legitimacy and international financial orders', *New Political Economy*, 12 (2007) and 'Everyday social sources of economic crises', *International Studies Quarterly*, 51 (2007). For examples of parallel and shared history, and global history seen from particular places, see V. Lieberman, *Strange Parallels* (2 vols: 2003, 2009) and D. Wright, *The World and a Very Small Place in Africa: A History of Globalization in Niumi, the Gambia* (3rd edn, 2010).

INDEX